Intersections

With Christ
at the
Crossroads of Life

Intersections

With Christ
at the
Crossroads of Life

Raymond C. Ortlund

WORD BOOKS
PUBLISHER
WACO, TEXAS

ISBN 0-8499-0127-8
Library of Congress catalog card number: 78-65798
Printed in the United States of America

To the Members of

LAKE AVENUE CONGREGATIONAL CHURCH

My own dear friends who
for twenty years have given me
the privilege of being their pastor,
I dedicate this book.

Contents

Introduction

Back in the last century and the first part of this one, Christians were engrossed in a new discovery of the Bible. It was a fabulous era. The second coming of Christ broke forth with new clarity, the "Keswick" teaching of the power of the Holy Spirit in our lives, and much more. Bible schools were born, as were Bible colleges, Bible churches, and Bible conference grounds. No wonder missions multiplied; the need was urgent to take this wonderful Bible everywhere, as it said to do. Truth was examined and loved for truth's sake, whether it "applied" to our daily lives or not.

Of course, eventually Christians began to get guilty consciences, that they knew more than they were acting out in their lives. And the pendulum began to swing from propositional truth to relational truth. It's been a wonderful era, rediscovering the Body of Christ, learning honesty and openness with each other, becoming involved in small groups, and examining our spiritual gifts with which to help each other. And seminars by the dozens have sprung up, some of them attended by unbelievable numbers. We've learned how to relate to our wives, our husbands, our children, our parents, our neighbors, the milkman, the dog. It's been a good era.

But we're hungry. We don't know The Book too well. We're getting the feeling that we've been exercising too much and eating too little. We're tending to be spiritually thin and nervous and hyperactive. And just lately I've sensed among the Christians I know, a deep longing to get back to propositional truth: to get enriched with doctrine, to know all those wonderful things God has written for us to know. We want balance. We want to walk on two feet—grace and truth. We want to "grow in grace and in the knowledge. . . . "

So my aim in this book has been to give you truth, and to give you grace; to give you Bible study, and to give you application; to put the searchlight of close scrutiny on the great events in the life of Christ as seen in the Gospel of Luke, and then to discover our amazing identification with Christ—that each event that happened to him has also happened to us!

Identification with Jesus Christ is a mysterious and remarkable thing. Suppose I put a piece of paper in a book. Everything that happens to the book, automatically happens to the paper. I can give the book away to someone; he'll own the paper, too. I can wrap the book up and tie a string around it and mail it to Africa; the paper will go along. If on the way the plane falls into the Atlantic and the book sinks to the bottom of the ocean, the paper will sink, too. The paper is in the book, and whatever happens to the book, also happens to the paper.

In some mysterious way, this is also true of you when you are "in Christ." It's one of the most foundational of all Christian truths that when you receive Jesus Christ, the Holy Spirit places you "in him." And the identification is so complete that whatever happens to Christ, happens to you.

This book is to show his perfection and to see that he is leading you to perfection. It is to enjoy the pattern of his life and to see that his pattern is your pattern. It is to make you wonder at his awe-inspiring fullness and to see that his fullness is your fullness!

I have been helped by many books. G. Campbell Morgan's *The Crisis of the Christ* is a masterpiece of fresh approaches.

Most of all, I am overwhelmed at the magnificence of Jesus Christ. And when you see anew with me that as Hebrews 2: 11 says, "Both He who sanctifies and those who are sanctified are all from one Father," then may the writer and the readers be joined in continual praise to him!

1

Christ's Birth
and Your Birth

Luke 1:26–38

I

A few years ago the December issue of *World Vision Magazine* had a unique cover. On a dark background there was photographed a torn-out section of a newspaper—the vital statistics. It read:

Berline, Mr. and Mrs. Douglas, Pasadena, a son, Michael, Dec. 23.

McCall, Mr. and Mrs. Lawrence, Arcadia, a son, James, Dec. 24.

Patterson, Mr. and Mrs. Daniel, La Puente, a daughter, Elizabeth, Dec. 24.

Joseph and Mary, Bethlehem, a son, Jesus, Dec. 25. . . .

Luke 2: 7 reads so simply, "And she gave birth to her first-born son. . . ." So quiet, so normal, so seemingly one of many, . . . and yet that baby was the Son of God.

Isaiah, seven and a half centuries before, had called him the Wonderful Counsellor, the Mighty God, the Prince of Peace. John was to call him the Alpha and the Omega, because he is without beginning and without end, one with God the Father and God the Holy Spirit from before the foundation of the world and reaching to all the worlds and dynasties to come.

THE TOGETHERNESS OF FATHER AND SON

A boy was turning the pages in a book on religious art. When he came to a picture of the crucifixion he looked at it for a long time, and there came a sad look on his face. Then he said, "If God had been there, he wouldn't have let them do it."

The amazing thing that we read in Scripture is that God was there! He was there at the manger; he was there on the Galilean road; he was there at the cross of Calvary. "God was in Christ, reconciling the world to Himself" (2 Cor. 5: 19). Reconciliation is the whole reason Christ was born.

The Father and the Son were together "pre-world." We talk about B.C., but this is P.W.: pre-world! God the Father and God the Son were one, together, inseparable before the manger, before creation.

This concept of pre-existence is different from our own existence. Although there is a great deal of controversy about this subject at present, there is nothing in Scripture that indicates we are born with a life that has a past. Life begins for us when we are born. We are born with a life that has a future. We simply have a quality of eternity that goes forward but not backward. God says in Psalm 139 that he formed you in your mother's womb; he thought you into existence; you were designed by God as you were formed.

THE SON: DISTINCTLY DIFFERENT

We have a here and a hereafter, but Christ was different. He had a *before,* a here, and a hereafter. We need to be aware of this uniqueness of Jesus as we worship him. He is not just a very good man with unusual abilities. We're talking about the One who came out of all eternity past, the Creator God.

In John 17: 5 Jesus prayed, "And now glorify Thou Me together with Thyself, Father, with the glory which I ever had with Thee before the world was." Get the impact of that! No one ever said that before; no one could. There was everlasting glory in the relationship of God the Father and God the Son.

John 1: 1 says, "In the beginning was the Word, and the Word was with God, and the Word was God." I don't know what the word *beginning* means in this verse. It seems to reach back further than Genesis 1: 1 when creation began, which means that the Gospel of John begins further back than the Book of Genesis.

"The Word was with God" (John 1: 1). Here the word *with* has to do with the eternality of the Father and the Son. The Word was facing God; he was turned to God. Certainly there's mystery here, but at least we see that the Word and the Father were in unlimited, unrestricted fellowship.

ONE WITH THE FATHER

But there's more than relationship here, there's actual identity: "And the Word *was* God." Conflict arose when, later on during Jesus' earthly life, he began to claim this identity. John 5: 18 says, "For this cause therefore the Jews were seeking all the more to kill Him, because He not only was breaking the Sabbath, but also was calling God His own Father, making Himself equal with God."

These people could have said, "Wait a minute; we're related to God, too." But Jesus was calling God his Father in a different way, a higher way, a more intimate way, springing out of a previous personal relationship (John 8: 56–58). This was more than they could take.

Christ's Sonship, then, didn't begin with his earthly life. He did not *become* a Son; he *was* God's Son. In the very beginning the Triune God identified himself with the family relationship—a relationship "from whom every family in heaven and on earth derives its name" (Eph. 3: 15). Every father's title goes back to God. This doesn't mean he is God, but it does mean that he is God's special, named representative to his family. He must take that role very seriously! Fathers of the church must also take their role in great earnestness, remembering that that relationship goes back to what the first person of the Trinity called himself from the beginning: "Father."

And Jesus, uniquely, is his "only begotten Son." We read in Hebrews 1: 4 and 5, "having become much better than the angels, [Christ] has inherited a more excellent name than they. For to which of the angels did He ever say, 'Thou art My Son; today I have begotten Thee'?"

What day? The first Christmas! Finally heaven's curtains were parted, and God was "manifest in the flesh." Then Hebrews 1: 6 reads, "And when He again brings the firstborn into the world, He says, 'And let all the angels of God worship Him.'"

UNIQUE IN EXCELLENCE

Firstborn—that's a name of great dignity for Jesus. The firstborn Hebrew son was not necessarily the oldest (remember Jacob in Genesis 27, for instance, and Ephraim in Genesis 48: 8–20), but he was the most important. He was first in leadership and first in receiving the inheritance. So Jesus Christ would be first in all that new race which was going to come to God by the redeeming work he would perform.

And to make the circle even larger, Christ is called in Colossians 1: 15 "the first-born of all creation," the Leader of it all. To exalt Christ properly we are given a huge list of titles for him, but surely "firstborn" is one of his greatest.

Our culture celebrates whenever anyone does something first. I remember when the Atlantic Ocean was first flown over by Charles Lindbergh. I was four years old when Lindbergh came to Des Moines, Iowa, my home town, and there was a big parade for him. My cousin put me on his shoulders so I could look over the crowd to see Lindbergh. I never could see him! Everyone was screaming and carrying on, and I was saying, "Where is he?" As far as I know, I never saw Lindbergh.

At least I shall see Jesus! I know that, absolutely. And he

is the first of all firsts. He is even the "firstborn from among
the dead." He is leading all his redeemed ones out of the grave,
out through the resurrection, into the presence of God, because he is first. What glory there is in the name God gave his
Son—firstborn!

GOD IN HUMAN FORM

So God the Father and God the Son are related in all eternity. But coming into time, the relationship revealed itself
when God took a body—that was Christmas. We call it the
"incarnation." Jesus is God "incarnate." What does that mean?

You go to a shelf at the grocery store and find a can labeled
"chili con carne." What is that? That's chili "with meat"—
literally "with flesh." Or before Lent people celebrate with a
festival called "carni-val," meaning "meat, goodbye!" And
when God revealed himself he came "in the flesh"—God "incarnate."

When a thunder storm comes to our area at night, we suddenly find a little boy in bed with us. He's there like a shot
out of a cannon, out of his bed and into ours. He says thunder's the only thing he's afraid of, but it's a standing agree-
ment at our house. He's like the little fellow who wasn't
comforted at night by the fact that God was with him; he
said he wanted "somebody with skin on."

JESUS, THE REVELATION OF GOD

Well, transfer that thought to God's coming "with skin on"
to comfort and to bless. Without Jesus men tend to get a gro-
tesque view of God. They think of him like themselves, only
larger. How do many people in primitive areas see God? They
picture him by their idols. He's a sensuous God to some of
them, because they are like that. Then they make their god
need all kinds of ugly and vile ceremonies. Or some picture
God as lazy, because they're lazy; perhaps they can't get God
to do what they want him to do. Or they picture him as greedy,
or vindictive. They need Jesus to come and tell them what
God is like.

In the very middle of Trafalgar Square in London is a pillar, and on top of it is a statue of Lord Nelson. It's up so high that you can see none of the features of Lord Nelson at all. In 1948 an exact replica of the statue was put down at eye level, so that everyone could see it at close range. And that's what God did at Christmas! He came down from exalted heaven to show us what he is like—in Jesus, at eye level.

A HOUSING FOR GOD'S PRESENCE

He entered into time as God incarnate, and he "tabernacled" on earth for a few years: "And the Word became Flesh, and dwelt [or tabernacled] among us, and we beheld His glory, glory as of the only begotten from the Father, full of grace and truth" (John 1: 14).

That word *tabernacle* is an interesting one; it comes out of the Old Testament. Remember when God ordered his people to have a temporary worship place while they were in the wilderness? Moses was given directions for building the tabernacle. It was a beautiful tent in which to house the very Presence of God.

Why does John 1 say that Christ tabernacled among us? Well, there are many similarities. The tabernacle was rough on the outside, but gloriously beautiful on the inside, with God's hidden presence. Our Lord Jesus Christ seemed poor and rough, but inside the poverty of that body there was the glory. "We beheld His glory," said John, referring to the Transfiguration of Jesus, the one time when that inner glory was allowed to be exposed.

The tabernacle in the wilderness was a place where God would meet with his people. And when Jesus tabernacled on earth, it was so that man could meet with God.

The Old Testament tabernacle was among the people of Israel for only about thirty-five years. So was our Lord.

The tabernacle didn't stay in one place like a permanent temple, but it went wherever the people went. And Jesus didn't even have a place to lay his head. He was a man on the move, for the people's sake. He tabernacled among us; he had no permanent dwelling place. He didn't make people come to him; he went to them.

God among us! What a miracle! It had been planned for all eternity. It was for your redemption, and for mine. The ramifications of that birth are enormous and are by no means all worked out yet. "God was in Christ, reconciling the world unto Himself."

How It All Happened

And specifically, what happened? Let's read the story.

Luke 1: 30–33: "And the angel said to her, 'Do not be afraid, Mary; for you have found favor with God. And behold, you will conceive in your womb, and bear a son, and you shall name Him Jesus. He will be great, and will be called the Son of the Most High; and the Lord God will give Him the throne of His father David; and He will reign over the house of Jacob forever; and His kingdom will have no end.'"

The angel said amazing things: that Mary would conceive— that would be a miracle. He predicted the sex of the baby and specified his name: Jesus. He said the baby would be famous, would be the Son of the Most High, would reign over Israel forever. And yet what surprised Mary the most was that she could have a child at all! "Mary said, 'How can this be, since I am a virgin?'" (Luke 1: 34). She was a pure girl, and she intended to stay that way until she and Joseph were married.

The astonishing answer came in Luke 1: 35: "And the angel answered and said to her, 'The Holy Spirit will come upon you, and the power of the Most High will overshadow you; and for that reason the holy offspring shall be called the Son of God.'"

The miracle was not actually in the birth of Jesus; I'm sure he had a normal birth. The miracle was in the conception, and this brief description makes us bow down with the shepherds and the magi and with the angels of heaven and with multitudes of saints past, present, and future. We fall on our faces in reverent awe.

THE ROLE OF THE HOLY SPIRIT

The New Testament calls the Holy Spirit "the life-giving Spirit," and Job said, "The Spirit of God hath made me, and the breath of the Almighty hath given me life" (Job 33: 4, KJV). It is one of his functions; it's what happens when the Holy Spirit is around!

The very first verse of the Bible announces that "in the beginning God created the heavens and the earth," and then says that "the earth was formless and void." What could correct that? Isaiah says that God "did not create it a waste place, but formed it to be inhabited" (Isa. 45: 18).

So Genesis 1: 2 tells us that the Holy Spirit immediately began his life-giving work: "And the Spirit of God was moving over the surface of the waters."

Those words translated *moving over* are the Hebrew equivalent to the Greek word translated *overshadow* in Luke 1: 35. The Spirit of God hovered over, he overshadowed the waters, as he would later overshadow Mary. And as he overshadows this shapeless, dead earth-mass, there comes out of it warmth, order, organization, and life! Because of the brooding over of the Holy Spirit, birds stir and twitter, plants sprout, cattle graze over the countryside, and fish flick their tails through sweetened, freshened waters. The miracle of life! That's what the Holy Spirit gives.

R. A. Torrey wrote, "The way in which Jesus was to be formed physically and literally in [Mary] is closely parallel to the way in which Christ is formed spiritually in each one of us." And then he quotes these verses: "My children, with whom I am again in labor until Christ is formed in you" (Gal. 4: 19). "That [the Father] would grant you . . . to be strengthened with power through His Spirit in the inner man, so that Christ may dwell in your hearts through faith . . ." (Eph. 3: 16–17).

Everyone of us who has spiritual life inside, in the person of Christ dwelling within, has been overshadowed at some time in our lives by the Holy Spirit, who caused this to happen! Amazing and wonderful!

SUBMISSION TO GOD'S WILL

So here was Mary, confronted with the angel's announcement. She could have done one of two things. She could have said, "Count me out, Sir. You're asking too much of me. Me become pregnant? Everyone knows we're not married. I just can't handle that."

Or she could have said, as she did, "I am your bondservant. Do to me as you wish." And from that moment on, when Mary surrendered her body to the will of God, the Holy Spirit was able to do his miracle work in her.

And her Son from heaven made an identical response to his Father's will: "That is why Christ said, as he came into the world, 'O God, . . . you have made ready this body of mine for me to lay as a sacrifice upon your altar. . . . See, I have come to do your will, to lay down my life, just as the Scriptures said that I would'" (Heb. 10: 5-8, LB).

And this is how God's will is always done. Mary said, "Here is my body. Do as you wish." Jesus said, "Here is my body, a sacrifice to you, Father." And to us comes the same call: "I urge you therefore, brethren, by the mercies of God, to present your bodies a living and holy sacrifice, acceptable to God, which is your spiritual service of worship" (Rom. 12: 1).

Study Questions

Review the text as you answer these questions.

1. Theology is the queen of all the sciences and never to be disparaged. It means the study of God. How many theo-

logical truths about Christ can you enumerate from reading this chapter? What difference do the theological truths about Christ make to you personally?

2. What does *firstborn* mean as related to the various functions of Christ?

3. In what ways have you seen the Holy Spirit operate in your life as he did in Genesis 1: 2 and following?

4. For the accomplishment of God's will, Mary surrendered her body, and Jesus surrendered his. In what specific ways can your own body literally be surrendered to the will of God?

II

We've been talking about the time, the moment in history, when God entered the human scene, and Jesus Christ was born. He didn't just ooze into this world; he was born, at a precise moment.

And God's Word says very clearly that each one of us needs an experience that he calls being "born again." We can't just gradually nudge our way into the Kingdom; we can't try to reform and eventually find we're in. It takes a moment in history which God calls our personal new birth.

Jesus spent a lot of time talking about this to a man named Nicodemus in John 3. Let's take a look at that passage. Backing up to John 2: 23–25, Jesus was in Jerusalem to celebrate the Passover, and while he was there, many "believed" seeing the miracles he did. But, according to the Living Bible, "Jesus didn't trust them, for he knew mankind to the core. No one needed to tell him how changeable human nature is!"

Apparently these people were convicted, but not converted. There's a great difference. It's easy to feel we know the Lord because we have a "head knowledge," but it hasn't gotten down to our hearts yet. Churches are filled with people who, if you asked them, would say, "Me, a Christian? Of course I'm a Christian. I believe in God; I believe in Jesus. I'm not a Hindu or a Buddhist."

That is what these people in John 2 would have said, but Jesus saw deeper than a "belief" which doesn't understand what true belief entails. Here the intellects were assenting, but the hearts and the lifestyles needed radical surgery.

NICODEMUS, AT THE TOP OF THE LADDER

Then we come to chapter 3, where we meet Nicodemus, "a man of the Pharisees." That phrase says such a mouthful, we have to stop and investigate. Because to this man Jesus was going to say, "You need to be born again." And if Nicodemus did, everybody does, because this man was a religious superman.

In Jesus' day there were about six thousand Pharisees, and they were the spiritual aristocracy of the day. Being a Pharisee meant far, far more than being a minister today. Today some denominations don't even require seminary training, and some have "boy preachers," maybe even an occasional boy wonder four or five years old who preaches, marries, buries, and all. It doesn't take much to be a preacher today.

But to be a Pharisee in Jesus' day actually meant that they had vowed to spend all their lives obeying every single law of Moses, plus thousands of other laws that they had added on to Moses' laws since his time. You can imagine how fat their book of rules was. There were twenty-four chapters just on how to keep the Sabbath. For instance, you could tie a knot with one hand on the Sabbath, but you couldn't tie a knot with two because that might be work, and you mustn't work on the Sabbath day.

The law of Moses said you couldn't carry burdens on the Sabbath, and through the centuries of refining his laws they thought, "Now, what does it mean to carry a burden?" So they decided that women couldn't wear brooches or pins on the Sabbath day; that would be carrying a load. Neither could you wear false teeth on the Sabbath! These and many, many more were part of the twenty-four chapters on how to keep the Sabbath, not to mention all the other rules.

We have to admit that if these Pharisees had vowed to keep all these laws—not just the Old Testament but so much more— they were some kind of religious zealots.

And not only was Nicodemus a Pharisee, but John 3: 1 says he was also a "ruler of the Jews." This is another way of saying that he was a member of the Sanhedrin, the Supreme Court of that time.

NICODEMUS' TEACHABLE SPIRIT

Both the Pharisees and the Sanhedrin were pretty threatened by the lowly Galilean who had come on the scene and stolen the hearts of the people, so it was actually a brave and rather unusual thing for this very important man to come to Jesus, especially with such a reverent and teachable spirit. He broke through all convention to come.

Is this why he came at night? Maybe, —although I must say, a man who tried cases all day and carried the burden of government upon him might only have had time to come at night.

And he said to Jesus, "Sir, we know that you have come from God, for no one can do these signs that you do unless God is with him." Certainly Nicodemus was up to the level of the people in John 2: 23—he was believing because of the miracles. (How wonderful when people are pricked to learn more about the Lord, and when they become aggressive in their hunger for him! Blessed are those who pursue!)

Jesus says to him, "Truly, truly, I say to you, unless one is born again, he cannot see the kingdom of God." Cannot even see, much less get in. Jesus cut through all of Nicodemus's credentials.

Nicodemus took Jesus so literally! This man who was an important teacher himself was also truly humble and teachable. He seemed totally dismayed as though to say, "You mean I have to do a re-run of my whole life? I have to back up and start over?" The very impossibility of it indicated he had no idea what Jesus meant, but he wanted to learn.

THE NEED FOR A TOTALLY NEW START

There is one miracle that Jesus never did: he never made an old person younger. He is not in the business of rejuvenating, of restoring the way you restore a cup that got cracked, of polishing things up and repainting, of fixing up the outside when the inside is the problem. He's talking about a completely different thing.

So he goes on to explain in verse 5: "Truly, truly, I say to you, unless one is born of water and the Spirit, he cannot enter into the kingdom of God." He can't see it, verse 3; he can't enter it, verse 5.

He's talking about the miracle of the new birth; keep that

in mind as we analyze what he's said. This miracle can happen any time in a person's life. At any age he can be reborn.

Recently a man touched my wife's elbow at church and said, "Come out to the curb; I want you to meet someone I've just led to Christ." She went out of the church, and there sitting in a car was a gentleman 102 years old! His skin was pink and fresh, and with his hornrimmed glasses on, my wife said he looked about 75, but his voice sounded like 150! In a faint little quiver he said, "I was thinking about heaven the other day, and thinking that I wasn't ready to go, and then God sent this fine young man along to tell me the way." Oh, the grace of God, that kept that dear man breathing for 102 years, until he was born again into God's family!

WATER AND WIND—WORD AND SPIRIT

But Jesus says we must be born "of water and of the Spirit." What he meant has been debated over the years. There's mystery here, and we want to tread carefully. It seems that the word *water* does not mean water baptism, because there's no miracle in that. As a matter of fact, there have been perhaps millions of people over the centuries who have been baptized by water but who were never born again. They experienced literal water, but not the new birth. There was no miracle there.

But water in the Scriptures is often a picture of the Scriptures themselves, and perhaps that is what is meant. Ephesians 5: 26 speaks of Christ's cleansing us by "the washing of water by the word." John 15: 3 says that we are clean by the word which he has spoken to us.

The next word Jesus uses is *wind:* that's the word for "spirit" in the Greek. It could have been translated that we are born "of water and of wind," which would have been even more mysterious.

Jesus hurried on, if not to explain *water,* at least to explain wind. He instructs Nicodemus not to be surprised at these things.

The Holy Spirit is Sovereign

In John 3: 8 he continues, "The wind blows where it wishes." Here Jesus says four things about wind to illustrate what he means by being born of the Spirit.

First, he says that the wind blows. This is a simple statement that affirms the ceaseless action of the Holy Spirit, always at work. We see him working in the Scriptures, from Genesis to Revelation. The opening words of the Bible are, "In the beginning God created the heavens and the earth." Then we find a situation of chaos and non-productivity, and immediately we find the Holy Spirit brooding over the face of the deep, working to bring life and productivity to it.

In Revelation 22: 17 the Holy Spirit pleads "Come," to anyone who will take the freely offered water of life. "Come to Jesus!" he says, still "brooding over" to bring spiritual life and productivity. Like the wind blowing, the Holy Spirit of God is ceaselessly at work.

Then Jesus says, "The wind blows where it wills," and it's also true that the Holy Spirit is sovereignly free. You cannot control the wind; you cannot control the Spirit. If you're a sailor you go with the wind—you tack, you do what you have to do, but you don't try to make that wind go with you. And the Holy Spirit does what he wants; he is sovereign; he is all-powerful.

We're Aware of the Spirit's Working

Then Jesus says, "The wind blows where it wills, and you hear the sound thereof." There is that indisputable evidence of the Spirit. None of us can see or measure him, and yet his presence in a life is so obvious!

For over fourteen years we lived across the street from neighbors whom we hardly knew. Our total relationship was "Hi, there" from one curb to the other. Then God's Holy Wind began to blow in their lives; first Dick was born again, then Betty. For the last two years we have been in a weekly small group with them; we've prayed together, laughed together, cried together, shared our lives and our hearts and much more. We've worshipped together thousands of times, and even sailed to the Holy Land together. There is a love between us that never existed before and which can only be explained by the work of the Holy Spirit.

The Holy Spirit gives an aliveness and an awareness that is unexplainable as the wind itself is unexplainable. But when the wind is present, you know it, don't you? You feel its presence; you hear its sound.

And so with the Spirit. When he stirs up a person there is no doubt that the work is going on. Or when he stirs up a church, how do you explain it? There are two churches; both believe exactly the same thing. In one church, though the creed is right, there is deadness. In the other church, believing the same doctrine, there is life, and people are coming to know the Lord regularly; Christians are happy and vocal about their faith. How do you explain it? Well, it's the presence of the Holy Spirit. You know he's there.

And this is what brought Nicodemus to Jesus; he'd been hearing the sounds of the wind!

Working from Unknown Sources

And Jesus says, "You hear the sound, but you cannot tell where it comes from." So it is with the Holy Spirit. There have been great movements of the Spirit. In 1750 both sides of the Atlantic Ocean were feeling a deep work of the Spirit of God. In our country from New England to Georgia, colonists were turning in large numbers to Jesus Christ. We call it the "Great Awakening," and it had a great influence on the shaping of our Constitution twenty-five years later.

But who can track down the source of these movements? How do they start? We don't know where the wind comes from, and this is also a mystery.

WORKING TO UNKNOWN CONCLUSIONS

And this verse says, neither can you tell where it goes. When you first accept Christ, you have no idea where his wind is going to carry you. When I first surrendered my heart to him at about the age of twelve, I never could have dreamed the marvelous adventures he would lead me through, as I was "led of the Spirit."

For Nicodemus, being born again was the beginning of a great life of being strategically important in God's plans. Like the rest of us, he had to stay "loose," he had to "flex," and not get rigid and unblowable. John 7: 48–52 (LB) tells about one of those later moments in Nicodemus' life. The Sanhedrin was in session, and one of the members said, " 'Is there a single one of us Jewish rulers or Pharisees who believes he is the Messiah? These stupid crowds do, yes; but what do they know about it? A curse upon them anyway!' Then Nicodemus spoke up. [Remember him? He was the Jewish leader who came secretly to interview Jesus.] 'Is it legal to convict a man before he is even tried?' he asked. They replied, 'Are you a wretched Galilean too?' . . . Then the meeting broke up."

Here Nicodemus was used by God to save Jesus from a premature death. His death was planned, but not yet. And in the very council chambers of Pontius Pilate, we have one of the boldest actions of the whole gospel story.

Then John 19: 39–42 tells how Nicodemus was used again, along with the wealthy Joseph of Arimathea, who was also a convert. Jesus had died; Joseph asked for his body, to put in a new garden tomb. "And Nicodemus came also, who had first come to Him by night; bringing a mixture of myrrh and aloes, about a hundred pounds weight."

So Nicodemus was strategic in Jesus' life and in his death.

SPIRIT-BLOWN DISCIPLES

Then there was the group of disciples. They had no idea

when they first got in contact with Christ that the Holy Spirit was going to blow them like scattered leaves around the world. It is said that Thomas went all the way to India, carrying the gospel! They could not have known their future. It's a scary yet thrilling thought that we must count the cost before we accept Jesus Christ and be born again, because forever after we are his, to be blown along by his Spirit wherever he has plans for us to go. But on the other hand, when he is the only One who totally understands us and who sees the overall scheme of things, who would want to go any other way?

Two Totally Different Spheres

Now we go back to John 3: 6: "That which is born of the flesh is flesh; and that which is born of the Spirit is spirit." Jesus says we must recognize the great valley which separates the flesh and the Spirit. There is an enormous difference here. Remember 1 Corinthians 15: 50, that flesh and blood cannot inherit the kingdom of God; or as *The Living Bible* says: "An earthly body made of flesh and blood cannot get into God's kingdom. These perishable bodies of ours are not the right kind to live forever."

The contrast between the flesh and the Spirit is enormous. Consider human birth: it ushers us into fantastic diversity. The act of being born can make us become a South Sea islander, or a European, or one who lives all his life on a boat in the waters of Hong Kong without ever getting off. We might have been born in a cave four thousand years ago, in a Greek palace in 100 B.C., the son of a seventeenth-century German schoolteacher, or in the twentieth century the daughter of Aristotle Onassis. We could have been one of those three precious babies born recently into a stone-age tribe in the Philippines—a tribe doomed to extinction until modern medicine came along. Human babies are born into such diversity, given all time and all space!

When we are born of the Spirit into God's family, we come into a unity that is simply incredible. We come into one family in the Spirit, and the family includes Abraham, Billy Graham, Jonathan and David—it's the same Holy Spirit of God within each one that unites all who have ever loved God and all who ever will. It spans all time and all space, all colors of skin and all cultures. Ephesians 4: 4–6 says, "There is one body and one Spirit, just as you were called into one hope of your calling; one Lord, one faith, one baptism, one God and Father of all who is over all and through all and in all."

When we have God in common, we are so meshed, it will take heaven itself for us to discover how united we are. It's an incredible union that transcends all history and all space; we are eternally and gloriously inseparable.

THE NECESSITY OF THE NEW BIRTH

There was a new pastor in a church who preached his first sermon on this seventh verse of John 3: "You must be born again." The congregation thought it was great. The second Sunday he got up and preached on the same text, "You must be born again." They wondered if he was absent-minded. The third Sunday he preached on the same verse, and by now they were all murmuring. After the fourth Sunday one of the church officers approached the fellow and said, "Pastor, why do you keep preaching on 'You must be born again?' " "Because," said the pastor, "*you must be born again!*"

A lot of evangelism must start in the church before it ever goes outside. Just as Jesus talked to a man so religious and influential as Nicodemus about the absolute necessity of being born again, so the Holy Spirit would urge every person alive in the same way: "Truly, truly, I say to you, unless one is born again, he cannot see the kingdom of God" (John 3: 3).

Second Corinthians 5: 17 says, "If any man is in Christ, he is a new creature; the old things passed away; behold, new things have come." *The Living Bible* says it this way: "When someone becomes a Christian he becomes a brand new person inside. He is not the same anymore. A new life has begun!"

The new birth makes you absolutely and totally different.

God no longer sees you in the flesh; you are in a new sphere, born into a spiritual family with God as your heavenly Father, and with all other believers as your brothers and sisters.

Marcus Dods, in *The Expositor's Bible*, said it this way: "For flying, it is not an improved caterpillar that is needed, it is a butterfly. It is not a caterpillar of finer color, more rapid movement, or larger proportions; it is a new creature."

And so God starts all over again with us, when we simply come to Jesus by faith. We discover that going to church isn't enough; being baptized isn't enough; joining a church isn't enough; reading the Bible and praying isn't enough. Though all these things are good and right, we must be born again.

Being born again is actually as simple for you to do as ABC:

A: Admit you're a sinner;

B: Believe that Jesus Christ died to take away your sins;

C: Confess before him and before others that you have received him into your heart and life.

God Will Do the Work

And then, just as the physical life of Jesus was miraculously placed in Mary, so the same Holy Spirit will miraculously place the life of Jesus in you. If he couldn't do that miracle at the first Christmas, he certainly can't do that present-day miracle we all want and need. In that case, God has no power, and none of us has any hope for this life or the life to come.

But millions over the centuries have "turned the world upside down" as they proved the power of God through the miracle of spiritual new birth. No wonder the Bible says the angels in heaven sing for joy over one sinner who repents!

> How silently, how silently the wonderous gift is
> given!
> So God imparts to human hearts the blessings of His
> heaven.
> No ear may hear His coming, but in this world of sin,
> Where meek souls will receive Him still, the dear
> Christ enters in.

Study Questions

Review the text as you answer these questions.

1. From Jesus' discussion with Nicodemus, what seems to make the difference between the millions in world-wide Christendom and those who have genuine salvation? Can you think of other parables or teachings which also show this difference?

2. Why isn't "doing the best you can" (like Nicodemus) enough to get you to heaven?

3. If by "water" Jesus did mean God's Word, why do you think he mentioned it as part of the process of the new birth?

4. When the Holy Spirit presides over lives, what difference will there be as opposed to the flesh's rule?

5. What do you see as our part in the new birth, and what is God's part?

2

Christ's Baptism and Your Baptism

Luke 3: 1–22

I

A bride puts on a wedding dress to get married. The priests of Levi, before they served, bathed and put on fresh linen robes. Before you do something special, you get ready.

The first event of Jesus' adult life was his baptism. Matthew, Mark, Luke, and John all record it. It was the launching pad of his earthly ministry. It was how he got ready.

Luke 3: 3 says that John the Baptist ". . . came into all the district around the Jordan, preaching a baptism of repentance for the forgiveness of sins."

Then verses 21–23: "Now it came about that when all the people were baptized, that Jesus also was baptized, and while He was praying, heaven was opened, and the Holy Spirit descended upon Him in bodily form like a dove, and a voice came out of heaven, 'Thou art My beloved Son; in Thee I am well pleased.' And when He began His ministry, Jesus Himself was about thirty years of age."

JESUS' EARLY LIFE

After the details of Jesus' birth, we are given very little information about his first thirty years. We have only two glimpses. One is the story of his visit to the temple as a twelve-year-old boy described in Luke 2: 41–51. The other is a pair of verses before and after this story which record his development. The earlier verse says that he grew in three ways: "And the Child continued to grow and become strong,"—physically; "increasing in wisdom;"—mentally; "and the grace of God was upon Him"—spiritually (Luke 2: 40). The later verse says that his growth continued in four ways: "And Jesus kept increasing in wisdom"—mentally; "and stature,"—physically; "and in favor with God"—spiritually; "and men"—socially (Luke 2: 52). Social development seems to emerge from the age of twelve on. But generally, these were years of seclusion and preparation.

Then suddenly, seemingly out of nowhere, Jesus appears on the scene and is baptized by John. Why was he baptized, and why by John?

THE IMPORTANCE OF JOHN THE BAPTIST

Let's think about where this was in history. Judaism had been in a long spiritual slump. For four hundred years there had been nothing but silence from God. There had been no prophet, no voice from heaven, no fresh word of God. Heaven's silence had been excruciating. The Israelites had been conquered by Rome, and it seemed as if none of God's promises could ever come true.

But as Hebrews 1: 1 says, "God, after He spoke long ago to the fathers in the prophets in many portions and in many ways, in these last days has spoken to us in His Son. . . ."

The Lord Jesus Christ broke the silence! His name was the Word, God speaking to men again at last!

But first, God sent John the Baptist to announce him, to be his forerunner. Just having the honor of introducing him made John the greatest of all the prophets! John became, then, the bridge between the old and new covenants, the Old and New Testaments. His word was that one was coming who was the end of all the millions of Old Testament sacrifices, the final fulfillment of all the thousands of Old Testament prophecies.

Now only a repentant, forgiven, cleansed people would listen to the words of Jesus Christ and comprehend what he was saying. So John's call was for Israel to come to repentance, and to prepare for the coming of this Messiah, this Son of God.

Matthew 3:7 says that multitudes came to John for baptism. He was a very attractive personality. He was that morning star which came announcing the dawning of the sun, the coming of the Son of Righteousness to arise with healing in his wings. Then John was to fade off the scene, and his disciples would become Jesus' disciples.

Revival always begins with believers who get their lives together again. That's always the way to fruitfulness and blessing. The first Beatitude says, "Blessed are the poor in spirit, for theirs is the kingdom of heaven" (Matt. 5:3). John's message is always needed; you and I need it at this very moment. The way to a fresh entrance of Jesus into your life, a new beginning again with him, is to humble your heart and confess your sins and seek his face anew.

REASONS FOR JESUS' BAPTISM

It seems so strange that Jesus would himself be baptized, as though he, too, needed to repent. Certainly it linked him publicly with John, and put his seal of approval on what John was doing. But his reason was more than simply to say that John was doing something important; Jesus, also, was doing something important. In baptism, though he was sinless, he was identifying with us sinners whom he came to save. I've heard it said that this was "guiltless participation in the collective defilement of mankind." Jesus came to save us, so he entered into our scene, even the scene of the people of Israel in their baptism.

Another reason Jesus was baptized was to "fulfill all righteousness," as Matthew 3:15 says. That is, Christ came to do every good work. He came to be the perfect Son of Man, to complete what a human should do in every detail. Part of that was being utterly identified with this remnant of sincere believers in Israel. Christ did that. He left nothing undone, to be the perfect sacrifice for our sins.

The good news is that all Christ did in his birth, in his thirty-three years of life, and in his death and resurrection, was for us! You see, he is not only our Saviour from sin, but our Saviour for life. He not only saves us from hell, but he gives to us his righteous life. He not only qualifies us for heaven, but he credits to our account his perfect earthly life for our earthly lives. He comes into us to live his life through us and becomes truly "the life" for us. He "fulfilled all righteousness," completed every bit of it in one human life, so that total righteousness could be ours by faith in him. Apparently, water baptism was necessary to perfectly complete that righteousness.

A PUBLIC LAUNCHING PAD

A third important reason for Jesus' baptism was that by it, he launched into his public ministry. John himself explained, "In order that He might be manifested to Israel, I came baptizing in water."

In other words, John's ultimate purpose was to declare openly Jesus Christ as Messiah and Lord, to announce his career, to draw back his curtain.

From this event, Christ moved out into his powerful, dynamic work. No one can follow Jesus in his baptism; it was absolutely unique, and for unique reasons. But all of us should obey his command to be baptized as well, and so declare ourselves for him.

If these are some of the reasons for Jesus' baptism, what were the results?

A UNIQUE COMING OF THE SPIRIT

First of all, he was anointed by the Holy Spirit for his ministry. Up to this time, for thirty years Jesus had heard the cries of the poor, yet he had not exercised his deity and his power to meet those needs. As far as we know, Jesus had heard the cries of the brokenhearted, but he had not attempted to solve their problems. He had seen the sick, but he had done nothing to heal them. Jesus had entered into no public ministry. But after his baptism, he went out and almost like a torrent of power upon the world, shared his glory, his deity, and his authority.

Before this time, Jesus had been one with the Father. He had been God the Son. For thirty years the Holy Spirit had been filling Him. There is no doubt about that. But something yet was needed before he could enter into his ministry.

At his baptism, that something happened. At that time "the Holy Spirit descended upon Him" (Luke 3: 22). Now, notice how he's described from there on: "And Jesus, full of the Holy Spirit . . . ." (Luke 4: 1); "[Jesus] was led about by the Spirit" (Luke 4: 1); "Jesus . . . in the power of the Spirit" (Luke 4: 14) . And then he walked publicly into a synagogue and read before them all, "The Spirit of the Lord is upon Me, because He anointed Me to preach the Gospel to the poor. He has sent Me to proclaim release to the captives, And recovery of sight to the blind, To set free those who are downtrodden, To proclaim the favorable year of the Lord" (Luke 4: 18–19).

"Well," we could say, "in earlier years he was filled with the Holy Spirit, too." Yes, he was. He was sinless and unique. But I see in his baptism a special coming of the Holy Spirit upon him which was a new enablement; it launched his career; it made him capable of being described in new ways, and it catapulted him into his public ministry. By his baptism he became ready for his particular, strenuous, powerful, redeeming three years, culminating in the cross, the resurrection, and the ascension.

And his baptism was all part of the predetermined plan. A thousand years before, the psalmist David had called him "the Anointed one," and prophesied the Father's words out of heaven, "Thou art My Son" (Ps. 2: 2, 7).

While in the Midst of Prayer

How was Jesus anointed? Let's look at the events that took place. First, we see that he was in the attitude of prayer. "While He was praying . . ." (Luke 3: 21).

I am deeply concerned that so many of God's people are not people of prayer! You know, we can do a lot of things without prayer, but we can't do anything meaningful or powerful until we pray. And we can do a lot more than pray, but it all begins with prayer. Prayer is not easy for me. I struggle; I push. While I cry to God that I want to pray, I seem to have a lag in my soul that doesn't want to! But as I look back over my life, I see that all the significant, lasting things that have happened have come about through prayer. May God keep me at it!

A fine surgeon and I were having lunch some time ago, and he said to me, "You know, I had a surgery to do that was very delicate. This surgery had been attempted twice before, and it hadn't been successful. I brought in famous people to help me with it. But the thing that made the difference," he said, "was that that morning my wife and I held hands, and we prayed together for that surgery. We asked God to help me and to guide my hands. And it was just marvelous! I was 'way beyond myself.' The surgery was a wonderful success."

And then he said to me, "I don't know why I haven't prayed more often." And all I could do was agree with him.

Peter Dyneka, that famous missionary to the countries surrounding Russia, says in his accented English, "No prayer, no power; little prayer, little power. Much prayer, much power!"

The Father's Voice

The second event leading to Jesus' anointing was an unprecedented act of God. He spoke to his Son out of heaven, saying, "Thou art My beloved Son, in Thee I am well pleased" (Luke 3: 22). It seems as though Jesus knew what was ahead

for him in suffering and hardship, and the Father comforted
him with encouraging words.

I remember one night I had driven across Los Angeles to a
rest home where one of our older church members was living. I was feeling very discouraged. It seemed as if the seams
in my life were all coming loose, and I was having a terrible
time. After I had called on this elderly lady, I sat under a street
light on the hood of my car, and I said, "Lord, I'm not going
home unless you give me something from your Word. I'm
desperate. I have to have a word from you. I need to hear your
voice. I need to know you are there. I need to know I'm not
alone." There were tears in my eyes, and I was talking out
loud. I don't know if anyone passed by to see me, but I didn't
care. With my little New Testament and Psalms in my hand
under that street light, God guided me to the twenty-seventh
Psalm. And God spoke to me out of his Word! "The Lord is
my light and my salvation; . . . The Lord is the strength of
my life. . . . For in the time of trouble he shall hide me in
his pavillion: in the secret of his tabernacle shall he hide me"
(Ps. 27: 1, 5, KJV).

THE SKIES WERE PARTED

And apparently simultaneous with the Father's words, the
heavens opened! I don't know how this happened, but the
event was so great that heaven and earth participated in it together, and Jesus was both physically and spiritually baptized,
all at once. The next time Scripture shows the heavens being
opened is for the Apostle John in the Book of Revelation. And
there seated on the throne in heaven is Jesus Christ himself!
He is "the Lamb, sitting," and all the beings of heaven cast
their crowns at his feet, rejoicing and praising and enjoying
him, because by that time he has gained our grace. Heaven
opened at the beginning of Jesus' work, and heaven opens at
the end. There is a dramatic, glorious awareness in all heaven
of what Jesus came to do and to be.

Then verse 22 says that the Holy Spirit came and descended

upon him as a dove. A dove is a gentle creature. Jesus said later on that we're to be wise as serpents, but harmless as doves.

Think back to the time when Noah sent out a dove from the ark to find a place to land, and it came back because there was no place. Someone has suggested that all through the Old Testament era the Holy Spirit was like a dove, seeking a place for a permanent rest, and not finding any. It's true that as you look through the Old Testament you see the Holy Spirit coming upon people and then leaving again.

But at last, here, the Holy Spirit found a permanent resting place—in Jesus. Jerome, the great translator of the Bible into Latin, quotes Isaiah 11: 2: "And the Spirit of the Lord will rest upon Him—the Spirit of wisdom and understanding, the Spirit of counsel and strength, the Spirit of knowledge and the fear of the Lord." Then Jerome goes on to say, "This prophecy was fulfilled here in Luke 3: 22. It came to pass that when the Lord had ascended from the water, the whole fountain of the Holy Spirit descended and rested upon Him and said to Him, 'My Son, in all the prophets I looked for Thee that Thou mightest come, and I might rest in Thee; for Thou art My rest. Thou art My Son, My First-born, Who art King forevermore.' "

Of course, there is a marvelous truth that because we Christian believers are identified with Christ and share his privileges, now we, too, are the permanent resting places of the Holy Spirit! In John 14: 16 Jesus said that the Holy Spirit would come to us: "And I will ask the Father, and He will give you another Helper, that He may be with you forever." Certainly to the disciples that must have been a startling and glorious new truth.

THE BONUSES OF HIS BAPTISM

Here is G. H. C. McGregor's summary of the baptism of Christ:

> He was always well-pleasing to the Father. But I cannot read my New Testament without feeling that

after this wonderful gift of the Spirit, His knowledge of the Father, His love to the Father, His sympathy with the Father's purpose, His delight in the
Father's will were deeper and stronger than ever.
There was, of course, no change in His character, but
there was growth, and it was this that fitted Him for
His work. It was in virture of what He became
through His anointing at His baptism that He was
able to do what He did.

For thirty years, all Jesus did and thought was a delight to
the Father. And God could say, "I am well pleased." But now
he needed this special work of the Holy Spirit to prepare him
for these three years of ministry, his death, and his resurrection.

This covering with the Spirit, this public authenticating by
the Father, this baptism of Jesus, was his launching pad, and
it was a stupendous event in his life. Without it he could not
have gone on. Hebrews 9: 14 tells us that it was "through the
eternal Spirit" that "he offered Himself without blemish to
God." All that he did was through the Spirit.

And, wonder of wonders, Jesus said that now he gives the
Holy Spirit without measure to those who come to him!

Study Questions

Review the text as you answer these questions.

1. In what ways was John the Baptist the bridge between the Old and New Testaments?

2. In what ways does Jesus' baptism seem necessary?

3. How and where do you see the other persons of the Trinity authenticating the life of Jesus?

II

Your identification with Christ includes a fabulous experience of personal baptism. It's so fabulous, in fact, that it's no wonder the devil uses this subject almost more than any other to divide and confuse Christians. This issue has been used to keep us "baby Christians." Hebrews 6: 2 says that "the doctrine of baptisms" or "instructions about washings" is baby food, and that if we're still wrestling with that one, we're immature. It says we need to get it settled and move on to other things. Let's pray that this study will settle some of the questions in our minds!

MANY TYPES OF BAPTISM

There are at least twelve kinds of baptism in the Scriptures. There are 106 references to baptism in the New Testament alone! But we can boil them all down to three categories:

1. *Figurative baptism:* as, for instance, Israel's national baptism with Moses in 1 Corinthians 10: 1–4, when Israel didn't get wet in the Sea at all; the Egyptians got wet; and yet it was Israel that was baptized! Or like Noah and his family in 1 Peter 3: 20, 21, who were never touched by the water, but the ungodly around them were immersed and lost! So the "baptism that saves" in these cases must be something else besides water.

2. Then there's *ritual baptism,* with water. John the Baptist made this kind famous, but the fact that from the birth of the church on it was still used, makes us know it's still valid for us. The early believers all through the Book of Acts used it for public testimony, and Jesus instructed us to baptize, in Matthew 28: 18–20.

SEEK FOR UNITY

Nevertheless, in the seventy-three references to the ceremony of water baptism, not a single one describes the specific way it was done. Even when the Scripture says they came "up out of" the water, the preposition could just as well be "away from." My dear friend, let me plead for us to give our brothers freedom here to follow the Lord's guidance for them individually. The psychological effect of plunging all the way under water in immersion makes it a wonderful form. But remember that millions in the great mainstream of believers through twenty centuries, both Catholic and Protestant, have used less water than that. Luther, Wesley, Calvin and many other of God's "greats" plus all of their followers have sprinkled or poured. "Let each man be fully convinced in his own mind" (Rom. 14: 5). The point is that literal water has been used, following early church tradition, as a visible sign of the inward work of needed cleansing.

I remember in my seminary days of a story going around among the Presbyterians. A Presbyterian pastor says to a Baptist, "If I immerse somebody just up to his ankles, is that enough?"

"No," says the Baptist.

"What if I get him wet up to his knees, will that do?"

"No, it won't."

"Up to his waist?"

"No."

"His shoulders?"

"No."

"You mean I have to get the water over the top of his head?"

"That's right," says the Baptist.

"Good," says the Presbyterian. "That proves that it's the top of the head that's the important part to get wet."

Well, it may get a momentary laugh, but actually, such little barbs and jibes have kept brothers divided over the years.

Relax about the age of the baptized, too! If God had wanted to specify a particular age for being baptized he could have easily done so. But the fact is that he did not. We must allow our fellow Christians to establish their own opinions in regard to this issue. "Therefore let us not judge one another any more" (Rom. 14: 13).

BAPTISM WITHOUT WATER

3. *Real* or *spiritual baptism* again falls into two categories, and these two have been terribly confused by Christians through the generations.

The first kind of spiritual baptism, Christ's baptism with the Holy Spirit, was foretold by John: "As for me, I baptize you in water for repentance; but He who is coming after me is mightier than I, . . . He Himself will baptize you with the Holy Spirit and fire" (Matt. 3: 11).

Then it was foretold by Christ Himself, just before he ascended: "For John baptized with water, but you shall be baptized with the Holy Spirit not many days from now" (Acts 1: 5).

At Pentecost it happened, and Peter explained that it had also been prophesied by the Old Testament: "But this is what was spoken of through the prophet Joel: 'And it shall be in the last days, God says, that I will pour forth of My Spirit upon all mankind . . .'" (Acts 2: 16).

Notice the distinctive peculiarities of this baptism. Jesus himself was the baptizer, according to John's description of it. There is no mention of the Body of Christ here. They are still in Judaism; they are still going to the temple. And it was for the purpose of empowering them to witness because of a very unique situation here in the first few pages of the church's history.

My friend, don't look for some mighty experience of wind, tongues, and fire on your head! Pentecost was a one-time thing, the birthday of the church, which can no more be repeated than Calvary. This was Christ's baptism with the Holy Spirit which he promised to those early believers.

BAPTISM FOR THE CHURCH TODAY

The second kind of real or spiritual baptism for us is the Holy Spirit's baptism of each of us believers into the Body of Christ. It is so wide, it reaches to all eternity, past and future.

It's so high, it is conceived in the heart of God. It's so deep, it includes the worst sinner, even you and me. It warms and fills us, the more we know about it. It's unifying and joyous! Listen to 1 Corinthians 12: 13: "For by one Spirit we were all baptized into one body, whether Jews or Greeks, whether slaves or free, and we were all made to drink of one Spirit."

If we believers have *all* been baptized, what kind of baptism is this? Not water baptism, or the thief on the cross could never have gotten into Paradise. The key is the first phrase of the verse: "By one Spirit." He is the only One who can do an everlastingly permanent work of truly baptizing all of us.

Donald Grey Barnhouse wrote in *Eternity Magazine* (Dec. 1951, p. 48), "The body of Christ is the whole invisible church. It was complete in the mind and heart of God before He ever created an angel or star. We will shine to His glory as the fullness of Christ, and in heaven the body will not be a mutilated one. We have His word for it: 'All that the Father giveth Me shall come unto Me' (John 6: 36). And you and I are in that body today, because in one Spirit we were all baptized into the one body."

There we have it. The real baptism is not into a baptistry—although that should be a precious experience. The real baptism is "into one body," the Body of Christ.

GOD's GENEROUS GIFT

Also if "we were *all* baptized into one body," then the baptism of the Holy Spirit can't be reserved for some special group of the "elite." And it is the only spiritual baptism for us today; there are not two: "There is one body, and one Spirit, just as also you were called in one hope of your calling; one Lord, one faith, one baptism, one God and Father of all . . . " (Eph. 4: 4–6).

Notice another distinction of this spiritual baptism: it was never prophesied in the Old Testament. It was a secret from all ages. Ephesians 3: 5 is Paul's explanation that it was a mystery which God made known to him by revelation: " . . . Which in other generations was not made known to the sons of men, as it has now been revealed to His holy apostles and prophets in the Spirit."

Another characteristic is that it is without sensation, without any accompanying experience, and without signs and visual demonstrations. "How silently, how silently the wondrous gift is giv'n... !"

But that's only on earth, within our very limited range of vision. In heaven God enrolls us in the Lamb's Book of Life, and all the angels sing and rejoice!

Translations of the Word *Baptize*

To understand how really wonderful this baptism is, we must look at the meaning of the word. The Greek word is *baptizo,* and primarily it means "to envelop." The noun form means "an element, which element has power to influence or change that which it envelops."

Or it refers to one thing being brought under the transforming power or influence of another thing. The old theologian R. W. Dale wrote, "Whatever is capable of thoroughly changing the character, state, or condition of any object, is capable of baptizing that object; and by such a change of character, state, or condition does, in fact, baptize it."

So according to the real meaning of the word *baptizo* we are not dipped into Christ to go in and out of him, but we are truly immersed, submerged, never to be taken out again. And the term also means to come under the power, influence, and leadership of Christ, not for a moment, but to be enveloped eternally in him. And so we are joined to him and identified with him and his work, unalterably and forever. Praise the Lord!

In this mysterious, mystical, and glorious way we are forever one with him and one with each other. And all he is and all he has done and all he ever will do is accounted to us. Now we can begin to understand the meaning of verses like Romans 6: 3, 4: "Or do you not know that all of us who have been baptized into Christ Jesus have been baptized into His death? Therefore we have been buried with Him through baptism into death, in order that as Christ was raised from the dead through the glory of the Father, so we too might walk in newness of life."

It's the work of the Holy Spirit to bring you to Christ and to place you in him forever. No ritual of men could ever accomplish this fact of making a poor sinner absolutely complete in Christ. And yet it's true, "In Him you have been made complete, and He is the head over all rule and authority; . . . having been buried with Him in baptism, in which you were also raised up with Him through faith in the working of God, who raised Him from the dead" (Col. 2: 10, 12).

THE GLORIOUS TRUTH OF BAPTISM

And now let us summarize all that we've said. We've looked at Christ's baptism, and we've seen that it was his preparation for ministry.

We saw that Christ's baptism was his enabling. Our baptism by the Spirit into the Body is also our enabling. And it's all the enabling we need. Wonderful! Our baptism is not some "explosion" later on in our Christian life—some experience we have, some feeling—although God will give these emotionally high moments from time to time as we walk with him.

But at our conversion, when we are placed forever into Christ, we get all we need for ministry and all we need for our lives through eternity. The Holy Spirit baptizes us into Christ forever with all the cleansing, freeing, enabling, authority, and power that that implies.

Think about it! Can you imagine what would happen if all the Christians of the world came to understand their true baptism? What if the glory of the truth of every Christian's oneness with every other Christian were exposed? What if we all saw together our oneness with Jesus Christ himself, thanks to the "one baptism" of the Holy Spirit, putting every one of us, small and great, into him? What if the clear truth of it hit us all at once together? All the confusion over baptism would be ripped away. All the division over baptism would be ripped away. We would be in the middle of the greatest revival the world has ever known.

No wonder Satan's special target of attack is baptism!

Study Questions

Review the text as you answer these questions.

1. Why do you think arguments over baptisms keep us immature, as Hebrews 6: 2 says?

2. Is water baptism necessary? Is it enough? Why?

3. What are the characteristics of Christ's "baptism of the Holy Spirit"?

4. What are the characteristics of the believer's baptism into the Body of Christ?

5. Describe how you know you have been baptized with God's "one baptism." Rejoice!

3

Christ's Temptations and Your Temptations

Luke 4: 1–13

I

Every Christian is tempted. Sometimes these strange temptations come like wave after wave upon us. You may have been in the surf at a Southern California beach when a huge set of waves has come in. You are out too far, and the undertow is too great, to get out of the surf. There you are, and the big wall of water comes in after you. You go for the bottom and grab sand, and you hold on. Then you come up and fight your way through a lot of foam, getting a gasp of air, and then there comes another wave just like the first one. Down you go, and hold on until you think the wave is over. You come up, fight your way through the foam, gasp for breath, and lo, another one is coming at you! At which point you begin to sing, "Lord, I'm coming home!" But eventually they let up, and you discover that you haven't died.

Temptation, at times, seems to come in waves. It did to Jesus. His temptations were a crucial part of his experience and life on our behalf. Let us examine the passage in Luke 4 on two levels: the persons of the temptation and the process of the temptation.

There are two persons involved in this temptation: Jesus and Satan. First, let us look at Jesus.

THE TEMPTED ONE

After his baptism, when he was inaugurated into his saving ministry, his first crucial event was to go through temptation. I believe there are three reasons why Jesus had to be tempted. One was to show to all the universe his impeccable character—his wholeness, his perfection. Hebrews, a book that speaks much of temptation, describes Jesus as "one who has been tempted in all things as we are, yet without sin" (Heb. 4: 15). His sinlessness could not have been clearly displayed if it had not been tested and proven.

Secondly, in his temptations he identifies with us in our temptations. We can never say that he doesn't know what we're going through. This also tells me that it's no sin to be tempted. Jesus was tempted! Even being "full of the Holy Spirit," as Luke 4: 1 says, Jesus was tempted to sin. Notice how strongly this is expressed for us: Jesus was "in the wilderness," but he was "full of the Holy Spirit," "led by the Spirit" (verse 1), and "in the power of the Spirit" (verse 14). Friend, you can be "in the wilderness"—in the atmosphere of this world—but at the same time be "in the Spirit."

VICTORY OVER SATAN

The third reason that Jesus was tempted was to defeat the devil. It's true that over the ages to come he will triumph over the Evil One. But in the midst of his earthly life, living in the nitty-gritty of human experience as do we, Jesus faced his enemy in hand-to-hand combat, and he won.

It wasn't that Jesus was anxious to go into battle. Luke 4: 1 says that he "was led about by the Spirit," but Mark's Gospel is even more forceful and says that he was driven. It was something he had to do, but it was an awful experience. It was so terrible that Jesus tells us to ask the Father, "Lead us not into temptation." And he warns us so carefully, "Keep watching and praying that you may not enter into temptation; the spirit is willing, but the flesh is weak" (Matt. 26:41).

But the great fact is that when Jesus had to face temptation, he went in victoriously, and he shows us how to make it through in temptation: by the use of the Scriptures. That's why we must know them well! We must immerse ourselves in them; we must memorize them.

We have two places of defense against Satan. One is being in the atmosphere of the Word of God, and the other is being in Christ. We have a kind of double fortificaton in times of testing. So Paul writes, "Be strong in the Lord, and in the strength of His might. . . . For our struggle is not against flesh and blood . . . " (Eph. 6: 10, 12). We have the Word of God in us, and we are in Christ, in that great fortress of safety. So we see three reasons why Jesus was exposed to temptation.

TEMPTED AS A TRUE MAN

We can't even imagine what a shaking experience this was for our Lord Jesus. In the first place, he must have become increasingly hungry and weak. He had no chance to eat before this staccato of onslaughts from the devil hit him. And anyway there was no food available in the desert, and he refused to make his own.

We must be careful not to think of Christ as some phantom, some unreal person. Sometimes that is done by well-meaning believers, but in seeking to elevate his deity we really lower his humanity. Even the great Godet writes, "Jesus' abstinence from food for six weeks was only the natural consequence of his being absorbed in profound meditation."

I have a hard time agreeing with that idea. He had a body like yours and mine. What happens to you when you miss one meal? Two meals? Nobody can live with you. You get cranky. What happens to your children before dinner each evening? It's just plain hard to get along with them, isn't it? Jesus had been through the depth of an experience with hunger that few humans have had, and he was, without doubt, in extreme exhaustion.

Greek mythology abounds with stories of gods who gave the impression that they were human, but when the need arose they cast off their pretense and used their revealed deity and powers. But our Lord was truly Man.

Forty days of temptation! Once I read the statement that Jesus "lived through life," and I think that's a good description of him. Most of us live portions of life—that is, we don't experience all there is to experience. But we find in Luke 4: 13 that "when the devil had finished *every* temptation, he departed from Him." Jesus lived through every temptation.

"THE ACCUSER OF THE BRETHREN"

Now let us consider Satan as the second person in this temptation experience.

Not all of your personal troubles are caused by the devil. There was a little girl whose mother was chiding her because she was so mean to her little brother. She'd pull his hair, and then she'd kick him in the shins. Her mother said, "What made you do such a thing? Did the devil make you do it?" The little girl said, "Well, it was the devil's idea that I pull his hair, but kicking him in the shins was my own idea!"

For a long time there has been combat between the Lord Jesus Christ, the King of Glory, and the god of this world—the devil. We often think of the devil as a horned creature with hooves and a tail, the buyer of souls and the manager of hell. No wonder many people don't take him too seriously!

The devil is a real person—a sinister, rebellious person who hates God and who at one time rebelled against God. Jesus commented on this once, saying that he saw Satan "fall from heaven like lightning" (Luke 10: 18). The devil is not in hell, nor is he in charge of it. The terrible thing about hell is that God himself is in charge of it and has reserved it for the devil and his angels (Matt. 25: 41).

For a person to choose to join Satan in his rebellion against God is unthinkably disastrous. It's an eternal choice, and God calls it "death"—the deepest kind of death, eternal separation from him. But that is the easy, careless choice that millions in this world are making. The word *devil* means "a spreader of reports, a slanderer." He has lots of followers.

THREE AREAS OF TEMPTATION

Luke 4: 3, 6 and 9 show that Christ was assaulted in three basic areas; there were three kinds of temptations, because there are three basic lures in this world. 1 John 2: 16 lists them as the "lust of the flesh, the lust of the eyes, and the pride of life."

The first human beings were tested in these three basic areas. "When the woman saw that the tree was good for food" —that's appealing to the lust of the flesh; "and that it was a delight to the eyes"—it appealed to the lust of the eyes; "and that the tree was desirable to make one wise"—appealing to the pride of life—"she took from its fruit and ate . . ." (Gen. 3: 6).

These same three temptations came to Jesus.

In Luke 4: 3, we see Jesus tempted to lust in his flesh: "Tell this stone to become bread." You see the lust of the eyes appealed to in the second temptation, verse 5: "He led Him up and showed Him all the kingdoms of the world in a moment of time, and said, "I will give you all this domain and its glory . . . if you worship before me." Then third, the temptation to the pride of life is seen in verse 9: "And he led Him to Jerusalem and set Him on the pinnacle of the temple, and said to Him, 'If You are the Son of God, cast Yourself down from here.' "

THE "LUST OF THE FLESH"

Now let's go over the temptations in more detail.

The first temptation was for Christ to turn the stone into bread. "And the devil said to Him, 'If You are the Son of God, tell this stone to become bread.' And Jesus answered him, 'It is written, man shall not live on bread alone' " (Luke 4: 3–4).

Again, try to remember how desperately hungry our Lord
Jesus Christ must have been. Then the devil came at that
moment and suggested that he do what he was very well able
to do, for he knew he would soon feed five thousand and then
turn again to feed four thousand, both miraculously. The
devil seemed to say to him, "Claim your powers!"

Why was this even a temptation? It's no sin to be hungry.
In fact, hunger is a sensation God gave us to tell us that we
need to eat. But Jesus said, "Man shall not live on bread
alone." That is, Jesus was saying that he was waiting not for
a word from the devil, but for the word from God, his Father.
The temptation was to think that his existence depended on
something physical and also to get that which he needed from
the wrong source. The temptation was to do the right thing
at the wrong time, at the wrong person's suggestion. But Jesus
never used his supernatural power for himself, for his own
personal need or ease.

Jesus quoted from Deuteronomy 8: 3. Bread is something
we live on, but not bread alone. Bread is good, but the will
of God is best. The devil continually wants you to choose the
good instead of the best. Jesus is saying that no true, full living
will ever take place on bread alone, but by the Word of God,
by "every word that proceeds out of the mouth of God," says
Deuteronomy 8: 3. And Jesus later said, "My meat is to do the
will of him that sent me" (John 4: 34). Friend, this is always
true with us. Remember that your greatest satisfaction is always in doing God's will! If you do God's will you cannot
lose. If you don't do his will, you cannot win.

THE "LUST OF THE EYES"

The second temptation is in Luke 4: 5–8: "And the devil
said to Him, 'I will give You all this domain and its glory;
for it has been handed over to me, and I will give it to whom-
ever I wish. Therefore if you worship before me, it shall all be
Yours.' And Jesus answered and said to him, 'It is written,
"You shall worship the Lord your God and serve Him only." ' "

Here Jesus got a panoramic view of all the kingdoms. Think of the Roman Empire at that time! It contained the kingdoms of Greece and Judea and Pergamus, Bosphorus, Syria, Egypt, and others. I like what Edersheim, the famous Jewish scholar, says about this temptation: "The world in all its glory, beauty, strength, majesty, is unveiled. Its work, its might, its greatness, its art, its thought emerges into clear view, and still the horizons seem to widen as He gazes, and more and more, beyond it still more brightness appears."

But you notice that the devil wasn't really giving up anything of his own. What he was saying was "Jesus, I want You to be my vice-president while I'm the president." This was an attempt at a takeover, kind of a spiritual coup. He knew Christ was going to be King, and so he offered a short cut around the suffering and the cross and the resurrection. He said, "Now, I'm going to give you all this without all that terrible experience, and you are going to be under me."

But Jesus was not after kingdoms. He was after *the kingdom* of God." Revelation 11: 15 tells of that momentous time coming when the kingdoms of this world will become the kingdom of our Lord and of his Christ, and he shall reign forever and ever!

So Jesus said in verse 8, "Nothing doing." In effect he said, "I will get the ultimate kingdom, not by your putting me in, but by my putting you out!" We sense a tremendous clash of forces between the God of glory and the devil—the god of this world.

THE PRIDE OF LIFE

The third temptation is in Luke 4: 9–12. Here, Satan "threw the book" at him: "And he led Him to Jerusalem and set Him on the pinnacle of the temple, and said to Him, 'If you are the Son of God, cast Yourself down from here; for it is written, "He will give His angels charge concerning You to guard You," and "On their hands they will bear You up, lest You strike Your foot against a stone." ' "

Satan not only quoted Scripture to Jesus, using Jesus' own tactic, but he took him out of the wilderness into the city. Not just any city, but the city of Jerusalem—the Holy City. "Oh Jerusalem," Jesus would say later on, as he wept over the city, "How often I have longed for you!" He loved Jerusalem. A thousand years before, King David had sung, "If I forget thee, O Jerusalem, let my right hand forget her abilities, her cunning!" The Jews always prayed toward Jerusalem.

So Satan took him to the Holy City, but not just to any part of it. He took him to the center of all their lives, right to the temple of God in the midst of the city. My friend, when you think about places where Satan can be, don't forget to include the church. There is no place and no time when we are not vulnerable to the temptations of the devil. There is no insulated place. Christian schools may be fine; but if you choose to send your child to one, don't do it because you think he will avoid temptation there. The devil will get at our children wherever they are.

THE TEMPTATION TO BE SENSATIONAL

Forty days previously, God's own voice had spoken out of heaven saying, "This is My beloved Son." Now Satan says, "If"—or actually the word could be *since*—"You are the Son of God, cast yourself down. Your Father will not let you get hurt, for he promises you protection. Go on, show off a bit. After all, it's a big kingdom you're working for. Get some visibility. A little P.R. won't hurt." He said, "Float down in dramatic fashion from the temple top. It'd be a big drop! The people could really have a splendid view."

Don't ever think that the devil is some weird creature in red tights. He quotes Scripture. He even suggests you do right things at the wrong time.

How Satan loves to tempt us to seek to be some spectacular kind of Christian who makes a big impression! Remember that the first Beatitude says, "Blessed are the poor in spirit, for theirs is the kingdom of heaven" (Matt. 5: 3).

"Humble yourselves," says James 4: 10, "in the presence of the Lord, and He will exalt you." Or as Peter repeats it, "Humble yourselves, therefore, under the mighty hand of God, that he may exalt you at the proper time" (1 Pet. 5: 6). It's on his calendar!

Jesus knew this, too. He could resist the temptation, and wait. There was no shortcut to bypass the cross, or suffering, or death. But the time would come when every knee would bow, and every tongue confess Jesus Christ as Lord, to the glory of God the Father (Phil. 2: 10–11). For this, he could wait.

VICTORY IN EVERY AREA

Then, as Luke says after the third temptation, "When the devil had finished every temptation, he departed from Him until an opportune time. And Jesus returned to Galilee in the power of the Spirit" (Luke 4: 13–14) .

He had begun in the fullness of the Spirit, and he came out the same way. He had come right through that gruelling experience unscathed.

Praise God for the victory of Jesus Christ on this threshold of his three-year ministry! It made him qualified for all that was to follow. If he had fallen into sin at this point, he never could have been our Saviour. He resisted, and he became victorious.

Study Questions

Review the text as you answer these questions.

1. How is it possible for a person to resist temptation?

2. Why was it essential for Christ to resist the devil at this time?

3. The lures of the world can be boiled down to three basic groups. What are they?

II

If Jesus Christ himself was tempted, we can be sure we will be, too.

A friend came into my study the other day. She was telling me how rough life was at that time, and finally she said, "Does it ever get easier? Do I always have this battle? Do I ever get to the place where I have constant victory?" And I said to her, "No, really, I guess you're going to go through testing and trouble all your life. This is not heaven." She said to me, "I don't know if it's worth it to carry on." And I said to her, "Well, what alternative do you have?"

What I meant was that this is the way life is: "In the world you shall have tribulation," said Jesus. God doesn't ask our permission first. Poor Job had it laid on him like a quarterback getting tackled from his blind side. That's the way temptations come—uninvited, without warning, and in every stage of life. If you think longtime Christians aren't tested and tempted ask an honest, godly believer. A saintly old man slipped up beside me in our church parking area. We were all alone and he said, "Pastor, pray for me. I am going through terrible temptation in my thought life." That seasoned veteran of faith had my sympathy because I know all about that kind of temptation too.

Testings and temptations are part of being human. Jesus said in Luke 17: 1 that temptations to sin are sure to come. I suppose that every one of us could say, "I believe that!" You never get so close to Christ that you are no longer tempted in multitudes of ways.

Now, all Christians are tempted just as Christ was tempted, because he so identified with us that he was tempted just as we are. Even in the garden praying, our Lord was tempted. Temptations followed him all through his life. There certainly is no reason for us to feel that we are not going to be tempted.

Again, what is temptation? It is not sin itself. It is the sug-

gestion to sin. Then let's ask another question. Who is it that
tempts us? Ultimately, the originator of temptation is the
devil.

TEMPTATIONS FROM THE OUTSIDE

Unhappily, I remember reading some Sunday school ma-
terial of one of the great denominations. It said, "A voice
within Jesus said this." It was no voice within Jesus at all. That
would mean that Jesus had a fallen nature; that there was an
evil side to Christ. There was no voice within Jesus! It was a
voice *outside* of him! It was the devil himself who tempted
him.

But the devil comes to us in many ways. He works through
our common needs, for instance—our natural, human needs,
not necessarily twisted by the fall, just the characteristics of
every human being. He came to Jesus through his hunger.

Or he uses secondary causes: he works through our fallen
nature, through what we call "the flesh." Or he's so subtle, he
will even use some very good thing God has given us to tempt
us to use that good thing in a wrong way.

Temptations are going to come to you when you are walking close to God. When you are undergoing devastating pres-
sures of life, and you sense that you are being pulled in pieces,
don't say, "How did I get out of the will of God?" Rejoice
that the devil thinks you are worth all that trouble, and cling
to God's holy will and his expressed Word. Or don't say,
"Well, I can't be a true Christian when all these terrible things
are happening in my life that I have to deal with—the temptation to get angry, to lash out at people, the temptation to
quit, the temptation to be afraid, the temptation to cry, the
temptation to give up. I can't possibly be a Christian." Friend,
that is sure proof that you are genuine, you are authentic.

If you are a Christian, you are going to face all sorts of
temptation. But as you walk with God, he's not going to leave
you. The Spirit who began your walk in Christ is the same
Spirit who will cause you to continue in Christ. Full of the

Holy Spirit and in the power of the Holy Spirit, Jesus went from his temptation. Praise the Lord!

Temptations come from outside of you, and temptations come from within you. A squabble between two of our city employees will not necessarily be settled by the president of the United States. In fact, you can be sure it won't be! It will be settled by the superior officer of the department in which the two work. Satan himself does not always give his individual attention to us. Remember, that he is not omnipresent. He assigns some of his lesser officers to us.

PINPOINTING TEMPTATION

But let's ask another question. If it's the devil who is the originator of temptation and of testings, then how are we tempted? What are the mechanics of temptation?

Turn with me to James 1: 12–15, and notice the steps in temptation. "Blessed is the man who perseveres under trial; for once he has been approved, he will receive the crown of life, which the Lord has promised to those who love Him" (v. 12).

Now, testings or trials are not necessarily temptations. But all temptations are testings or trials. Let me explain what I mean. In temptation you have a choice that you must make— to do God's will; or to do your own; to do good, or to do evil. But in testings you don't have a choice. You get thrust into a hard situation, and you're there. It may be a financial situation, or a difficult home situation, or an illness, and you have to go through it. The writer here speaks of the *blessedness* of testings.

Jesus' prayer for his disciples includes "Lead us not into temptation." Peter was the one who bragged, "Lord, though every one else deny you, I will never deny you. Whatever others may say, old Peter will stand right by you, Lord. You can count on me." Then, you remember, it happened! That's why Jesus said we should pray, "Lead us not into temptations" that are too much for us and will prove our undoing.

THE "PLUS" OF TESTINGS

But testings prove and improve us. Woe to us if we did not have testings which even involve temptations! We would be so weak! For testings, along with these temptations, really humble us, don't they? They teach us that we must seek God continually. They teach us never to trust ourselves. They teach us that we're in a battle, and if there's no warfare, there's no victory. Part of the Christian life is sheer, dogged battle.

The Scripture goes on to say this, "Let no one say when he is tempted, 'I am being tempted by God'; for God cannot be tempted by evil, and He Himself does not tempt any one. But each one is tempted when he is carried away and enticed by his own lust. Then when lust has conceived, it brings birth to sin; and when sin is accomplished, it brings forth death" (James 1: 13–15).

You notice the steps, here. Satan begins by using our natural needs—our desires, our lusts. Enticed by these, we go on to something else. Now, lust, or desire, is not bad in itself. The same word is used of Jesus when the Scripture says, "With desire have I desired to eat this Passover with you" (Luke 22: 15, KJV). Paul used the same word when he said, "I have a desire to be with Christ, which is far better." Lust isn't sin; it is desire within us, given by God, for food, for company of other people, for knowledge, for love—all of those things that are basic to life.

HOW DO WE GET WHAT WE WANT?

The issue is, how are we going to fulfill all of these desires? We can fulfill them in the will of God, or we can do them in our own way, in our own time. We can do them with the glory of Christ in mind, or we can do them through our own desires and imposed will.

Two words are used in this text, *lured* and *enticed*. The word *lured* or *drawn*, is a hunting word. A hunter uses a duck call and quacks away in his hidden brush to "lure" the ducks, and then he shoots them down. This is what the devil does with our natural inclinations: he "lures" us in to close distance, and then he shoots us down.

The other word is *enticed*. It has to do with a fishing bait. We get "hooked" by these naturally good desires of ours. It was not wrong for Jesus to want bread. When the devil said, "Let's work together on this, Jesus, and you turn this stone into bread," he wanted to let the end justify the means. Jesus could well have eaten bread. He was hungry. It was not wrong. But Jesus would not have bread by that means.

BY WRONG MEANS

So the method of the devil is to get a good man to fulfill legitimate desires in the wrong way. And he works that way on you, my friend. That's what we find in Eve's temptation. The very first temptation comes suddenly, treacherously, to this woman: "Now the serpent was more subtle than any other wild creature that the Lord God had made. He said to the woman, 'Did God say, "You shall not eat of any tree of the garden?"' And the woman said to the serpent, 'We may eat of the fruit of the trees of the garden; but God said, "You shall not eat of the fruit of the tree which is in the midst of the garden, neither shall you touch it, lest you die."' But the serpent said to the woman, 'You will not die. For God knows that when you eat of it your eyes will be opened, and you will be like God, knowing good and evil.' So when the woman saw that the tree was good for food, and that it was a delight to the eyes, and that the tree was desired to make one wise, she took of its fruit and ate; and she also gave some to her husband, and he ate" (Gen. 3: 1–6, RSV).

Notice that here she has just a brush with the devil, one of those harmless brushes. "Now the serpent was more subtle than any of God's created things." And we often find the subtleness of Satan in our lives. He says, "Don't worry about it. Just this once."

What's Wrong with Yielding?

"Well," you could say, "Didn't King David, that great veteran, earn the right to stay home from battle that day? Wasn't it his right to go up onto his housetop and look over the city? Wasn't it the right of David to have a little quiet luxury? He was a mature man. Couldn't he look where he wished? He was king over all those people. And if there was a maid over there, on whom he could look, wasn't it his right? And what's more, why wouldn't he have a right to this woman? He had risked his whole life for this kingdom, for this woman herself." So goes carnal reasoning, and so David fell. So subtle was the temptation! And he had time. . . . And she was available. . . .

What's wrong with fleshy, lusty magazines? We reason that "We have to know what's going on today. We need to see a few of these dirty movies or else how are we going to know how to deal with people in sin, if we don't have some idea of these things? And, after all, we are mature adults." My friend, you know all too well what's going on in this world, and you don't need any schooling. Neither do I; I am too well aware of it now. Oh, how subtly we can argue our way into that vulnerable position and be caught!

The serpent said to the woman, "Did God say you shall not eat of the trees of the garden?" He begins to cross-examine her and puts her on the spot. She begins to wonder, "What am I supposed to say now? Who is talking to me, anyway?" Where was Adam at that moment? She may have felt lonely, even helpless. Soon she yielded and then brought Adam down with her.

Yielding by Degrees

Temptation comes subtly. Friend, let me tell you that the evil one is on our backs, and don't you forget it. I know it all too well, and so do you. In this day, with all that we have, we have learned to live very close to the edges of sin. Sin has become a part of life.

Sodom was glamorous to the eyes of Lot. Life there seemed vivid and rich. From the bare Judean hills he could look down on this beautiful area. There was lushness, ease, the fruits of the earth there. Lot looked down upon it, and his family all agreed with him that they should go to Sodom. Surely Sodom couldn't do any harm to Lot and his family; they were believers! What's the use of isolating the children and keeping them from these things? They need to know what life is about. So down to Sodom they went, right into the middle of the city. Eventually the children married in Sodom, and that family had to be absolutely cut away from the city before God destroyed it. Lot went downward in successive phases of weakness, first pitching the tent toward Sodom, then going into the city, then becoming one of the very leaders of the city, and then his children being in the middle of city life.

How many people this has happened to in evangelical families? Parents have said, excusing their children, "It's very hard to live a Christian life in a time like this. It was different, you see, in our day. But now. . . ." So they let them go here, and they let them go there. And things that look very harmless, gradually become harmful. And many children are lost.

Think of the city of Gaza, a very glamorous place to Samson. The people were something like Europeans, with sophistication, art, philosophy, and culture. So Samson goes to Gaza among the Philistines. He gets away from those austere, narrow-minded Hebrews, and he thinks, "Just fundamentalists, that's all they are." He goes slipping down, time and again to Gaza, until he lives there, and he marries a girl there. And finally he ends up with his eyes put out, dead under the ruins of the city.

Successive temptations, successive falls, and then the end. The first step is desire. The second step is to be enticed and lured outside of God's will, and then, sin conceived, brings forth death.

WEAPONS AGAINST THE ENEMY

Perhaps at this very moment you are going through temptation. What can you do when you're tempted? Remember that while you're weak in yourself, you have tremendous fortifications. Jesus Christ is within you! The strong Son of the living God has redeemed you, and he places within every believer a new nature, with new desires and new resources.

And not only is he within you, but you are in him! You are surrounded by him, enclosed in him, ensphered in him—in his family, in his plans, and in his grip. "No temptation has overtaken you but such as is common to man; and God is faithful, who will not allow you to be tempted beyond what you are able; but with the temptation will provide the way of escape also, that you may be able to endure it" (1 Cor. 10: 13) .

How wonderful God is to give us ways to escape! How many times in my own life he has come in with a way of escape! Why? Because Jesus has promised us that he prays for us. Satan wanted to sift Peter like wheat, but Jesus said, "I have prayed for you, that your faith may not fail" (Luke 22: 32).

Dear friend, when you draw your strength from Christ, you have one praying for you whose prayers get right through to the Father! And they are very productive.

So when you are tempted:

1.   Call on Christ.
2.   Expect him to show you a way of escape.
3.   Take his way.

STAY TENDER

Another great preventative against sin is to be continually shocked by it. Never let yourself get hardened! It was sin that nailed Jesus Christ to the cross. Sin has broken the hearts of people through the years. Sin leads people to despair. Don't let it ever become "ordinary" to you. Eve only intended to taste the fruit. And so it happens with you. Just one little thought, one little deed, just a little conversation, you don't intend very much; you know how it goes.

But then Satan offers larger experiences, just as he did to Lot, to Samson. The years are passing, and maybe you're missing something, and he says, "Have a little more taste out of life. . . . " We're tempted; we all have feet of clay. The Bible says, "Flee youthful lust. Run from sin!"

A minister in San Francisco found himself suddenly in a position that was very difficult. There he was, face to face with a woman, with all the opportunities that he wanted in his own lust. At first he thought, "I will share some Scripture verses with her, and talk about Christ." But then he got sensible, and he ran!

C. S. Lewis in *The Great Divorce* wrote about temptations, "On the borders of heaven there was a poor wretch walking with a red lizard on his shoulder. An angel of light came up and said, "Let me break its back." The lizard whispered into the ear of the man, "Oh, no, no! The wonderful things I tell you, the images I pour into your mind."

"Let me break its back!" said the angel of light. "Oh well, go on," said the man.

The angel broke its back, and flung it on the ground, and it turned into a mighty stallion on which the man could get up and ride and gallop away."

When you withstand temptation and testing, God makes a real person out of you, and the results begin to be those things that guide you on. You can become one of God's great servants.

So, rejoice, when you go through testings and temptations! Do not feel dirty when you have temptations! Draw all your strength from the Savior and overcome by the blood of the Lamb.

Study Questions

Review the text as you answer these questions.

1. Is even the most godly Christian tempted? Why?

2. Describe Satan's forces and tactics.

3. Who is the source of temptations? What effect do they have on us? Who is the source of testings? What effect do they have on us?

4. Would you say that more temptations are obvious or subtle? Share some ways you've found to handle them.

4

Christ's Choosing of Disciples and Your Choosing of Disciples

Luke 6:12–19

I

Even in Jesus Christ's perfect life there were crucial moments—corners that he turned which produced new turns of events—and one of those times was the choosing of his twelve disciples.

It came in the very middle of his three-year ministry. For a year and a half he had called men from time to time, and they had told others, and the group had grown to perhaps hundreds of disciples. Jesus was now in a situation where he had more people around him than he could handle. Of course, he was the Son of God, but he had voluntarily limited himself when he came to this earth in a human body. And being "in the flesh," he got tired like the rest of us, could only be in one place at one time, and so on. He was not capable of discipling hundreds of people at close, intimate range any more than we are.

So at this point in his career he "eliminated and concentrated." He entered into a new and deep relationship with twelve men. This change meant, no doubt, a significant altering of his lifestyle; it must have even seemed to those who knew him like a shockingly new regime. It seems that new things rarely ever come easily.

PREPARATION FOR A REVOLUTIONARY THING

In order to prepare his followers for this change, he told an interesting parable just before he publicly chose the Twelve. He said you don't cut a piece out of a lovely new garment and sew it onto an old one, because it will pull away from the old. The old isn't strong enough to hold it. And he said, you don't take new wine and put it into old wine bottles. They will break, and the wine will spill out. And he made this wry comment: "No one, after drinking old wine, wishes for new; for he says, 'The old is good enough'" (Luke 5: 39).

You may have an old sweater that you like to wear around the house. Your wife would like to put it in the furnace and burn it, but you like it. She says, "Why don't you get rid of that ratty old sweater? It looks so bad, and those old trousers. . . ." And you say, "But, dear, they feel so good! 'The old is good enough!'"

That's the way it is with much of life. It's easy to feel comfortable with what we've always done. Jesus was calling twelve men to start with something fresh and new, which would require a fresh, new commitment. This was not like patching up an old garment; this was like putting on a whole new coat. Sometimes the new coat doesn't feel like the old one; it's kind of scratchy and uncomfortable. We're tempted to drift back to the old attitude: "the old is good enough."

Here it was time for change! Jesus said, "New wine must be put into fresh wineskins." "This is going to be revolutionary."

GOING DEEPER WITH A FEW

"And it was at this time that He went off to the mountain to pray, and He spent the whole night in prayer to God. And when day came, He called His disciples to Him; and chose twelve of them, whom He also named as apostles. . . ." (Luke 6: 12–13).

Out of many disciples or followers, perhaps hundreds, he picked the Twelve. He began to give his life in special ways to these men, to teach them, to care for them, to be with them.

The first half of Jesus' ministry was characterized by crowds, and he spent much time preaching, healing, feeding and caring for the multitudes. But the last and best half of his ministry was reshaped to give priority to these twelve men—and out of twelve, three. Over and over in the text you see the word *withdrew*. You find he taught the crowds in parables, and then he would withdraw to give fuller explanation to his inner circle. Whatever he did in public, he did with these men at his elbow, as they watched and listened and learned. It was at this midway point that the Twelve actually left their homes and from then on, for one and a half more years, were on the road with him, sharing his lifestyle, sharing his homelessness.

THE COST OF DISCIPLESHIP

After he called the Twelve, Jesus told them what their future was going to be like. Luke 6: 20 reads, "[Jesus] turning His gaze on His disciples, He began to say, 'Blessed are you who are poor. . . .'"

Now, remember that Peter was a pretty successful fisherman. And Jesus began saying "Peter, blessed are you who are poor. . . ." Peter probably thought, "Poor?" "Yes, that's what the future is going to be like, Peter." But then Jesus added, "'. . . for yours is the kingdom of God. Blessed are you who hunger now, for you shall be satisfied. Blessed are you who weep now, for you shall laugh. Blessed are you when men hate you, and ostracize you, and heap insults upon you, and spurn your name as evil, for the sake of the Son of Man. Be glad in that day, and leap for joy, for behold, your reward is great in heaven'" (Luke 6: 20–23).

Up to this moment the Twelve had been part of his larger group of disciples—a "multitude," they're called, who no doubt tended to gather with him at all public occasions but who nevertheless had their own homes, businesses, and families. You remember that Jesus went to Peter's home to visit him, and while there, cured his mother-in-law. After Matthew was con-

verted, Jesus went to Matthew's home. And the two disciples
mentioned in John chapter 7 went home with Jesus to his
own house, no doubt the one he shared with his mother and
brothers and sisters.

But after this crucial point, the Twelve truly "left all," and
followed him permanently. He left his home; they left theirs.
"The foxes have holes," Jesus was to say later, "and the birds
of the air have their nests; but the Son of Man has nowhere
to lay His head" (Matt. 8: 20). And Peter was to say, "Behold,
we have left our own homes" (Matthew and Mark say "everything") "and followed You." And Jesus answered, "Truly I
say to you, there is no one who has left house or wife or brothers or parents or children, for the sake of the kingdom of God,
who shall not receive many times as much at this time and in
the age to come, eternal life" (Luke 18: 28–30).

If we had been onlookers in that day we might have thought,
"Well, too bad for those fellows. They are through! They are
in for a hard life, and this is probably the last we'll hear of
them."

Of course, it wasn't the last at all; it was the way to greatness. "And behold, some are last who will be first" (Luke 13:
30). The way to up is down. Ephesians 2: 20 reveals to us that
the living, eternal church of Jesus Christ is forever built upon
"the foundation of the apostles and prophets." Talk about un-
dying status! And we find that these men became many of the
writers of the New Testament: they were moved by God's
Holy Spirit to become human authors of his precious Word.
Furthermore, Rev. 21: 14 says that the walls of the eternal
city, the New Jerusalem, have twelve foundation stones, and
on them are the names of the twelve apostles of the Lamb. All
through eternity the names of the Twelve will be there, for
all to see. I would say that these men made the right choice.
And evidently Jesus thought so, too.

A TRUE "CRUX"

The choosing of the Twelve was a momentous event for

all history to come. That's why I say that this was one of the turning points in Christ's life. I want you to see how carefully he entered this new era, and yet how simple was his plan.

Elton Trueblood, in his book *The Lord's Prayers,* says, "It is no exaggeration to say that Christ's decision to select the Twelve was one of the most crucial decisions of the world. There is no reason to suppose that we should ever have heard of the Gospel apart from this carefully conceived step. Since Christ wrote no book, he depended entirely upon the faithfulness of the prepared group. Not all of them understood him or proved faithful; yet in the end, the method succeeded."

First let's see how Jesus used the old way of prayer and the new way of discipleship for his future, his new way of ministry.

BEHIND THE SCENES

The old way was a careful decision by prayer: "And it was at this time that He went off to the mountain to pray, and He spent the whole night in prayer to God" (Luke 6: 12).

By example and by word, Jesus taught us to face every crisis with prayer. Your own future is too precious to do otherwise! Someone once said, "Life is like a parachute jump. New learners must be taught to get it right the first time!" The answer to the "how" of life is prayer.

At Jesus' baptism, "While He was praying, heaven opened. . . ." At his transfiguration, "While He was praying . . ." he was transfigured. In the Garden of Gethsemane before his arrest, "He knelt down and began to pray." Before each major event of his life, not panic but prayer. And here, before choosing his inner circle of disciples, Jesus spent the night in unbroken quietness with the Father.

Oh, my friend, learn this discipline! Work prayer into the very fabric of your days and of your life, of your planning and of your thinking. You see, there is prayer, and then there is *prayer.* And Jesus at this point was *praying.* There must be times when you leave everything else and linger with God, to spend time alone with him. How important it is to have times

of discovering new directions with God! Take your datebook,
take a hymnbook, take your Bible, and go away to be alone.
Read the Word; look over where you are in your life; jot down
what the future looks like. Pray it over; think it through.

That's what Jesus was showing us here. He spent the whole
night in prayer. In fact, those words "He spent the whole
night" are actually one Greek word. This is the only place it's
used in all the Greek New Testament, and it's in a form that
would tell us that he persevered. He gave himself in prayer.
And the phrase "prayer to God" is really not prayer *to* God
but in the Greek, prayer *of* God. I don't know what all that
means, but I think it means that he was involved in the presence of the Father. He was in holy communion with God.

In that communion, God gave him the names of the men
he was to choose to be his disciples. In John 17: 6, that high-
priestly prayer of Jesus, he mentioned two times "the men
whom Thou gavest Me." They were in answer to his prayers.

A New Method For His Message

Secondly, Jesus not only relied on the old way of prayer,
but he launched his new type of operations. The result of
that night of prayer is seen in Luke 6: 13: "When day came,
He called His disciples to Him; and chose twelve of them. . . ."

It made a new beginning in his style of interpersonal relationships. Notice in this sixth chapter of Luke the concentric
rings of people around Jesus following his choosing of the
Twelve. Verse 13 says he called his disciples *to Him* and descended the mountain *with them;* they were now the inner
circle closest to him. Verse 17 says that, descending the mountain, he stood on a level place with his Twelve at his elbow,
and "a great multitude of disciples"—no doubt the remaining
followers who had been with him in the mountain—were ring-
ing about him. Outside this circle of perhaps hundreds were
the curious: ". . . a great throng of people from all Judea and
Jerusalem and the coastal region of Tyre and Sidon, who had
come to hear Him, and to be healed of their diseases; and

those who were troubled with unclean spirits were being cured. And all the multitude were trying to touch Him, for power was coming from Him and healing them all" (Luke 6: 17–19).

The Living Bible makes the picture even more clear in verses 17 and 18: "When they came down the slopes of the mountain, they stood with Jesus on a large, level area, surrounded by many of his followers who, in turn, were surrounded by the crowds."

The new areas of Jesus' concern in ministry were his Twelve, his other followers (soon he would send seventy out, two by two), and the uncommitted crowds—still and always the object of his love and compassion.

ELIMINATING TO CONCENTRATE

But notice the vast difference in the relationships here. The crowds, in verse 19, expressed typical "crowd reaction": "Everyone was trying to touch Him. . . ." Crowd reaction is always superficial and emotional: touch will suffice.

Jesus' relationship with his disciples was altogether different. He turned and taught them. He met them on the level of their minds, their hearts, their intellects, their emotions, their wills—their whole persons. He got to them deeply, totally.

Don't be a "fringe Christian," content to be part of a crowd getting a "touch" of Jesus! Instead get in the "inner circle." Be satisfied with nothing less than to be deeply taught and deeply changed.

"And turning His gaze on His disciples, He began to say . . ." (Luke 6: 20). The message was for all the hearers, but Jesus had a new concern, a new love in his life, the precious ones at his elbow who were to develop under his special tutelage.

From here on, you can picture the situation: ". . . He went to a city called Nain; and His disciples were going along with Him, accompanied by a large multitude" (Luke 7: 11). "And . . . He began going about from one city and village to another, proclaiming and preaching the kingdom of God; and the twelve were with Him" (Luke 8: 1). "Now it came about on one of those days, that He got into a boat, He and His disciples, and said to them, 'Let us go over to the other side of the lake . . .'" (Luke 8: 22). The new life style was launched!

The Cost Is Worth It

Juan Carlos Ortiz's book, *The Disciple*, talks about Jesus as the Pearl of great price. Here's a conversation that goes on about buying the Pearl:

> "I want this pearl. How much is it?" "Well," the seller says, "it's very expensive." "But, how much?" we ask. "Well, a very large amount." "Do you think I could buy it?" "Oh, of course, everyone can buy it." "But, didn't you say it was very expensive?" "Yes." "Well, how much is it?" "Everything you have," says the seller. We make up our minds. "All right, I'll buy it," we say. "Well, what do you have?" he wants to know. "Let's write it down." "Well, I have ten thousand dollars in the bank." "Good—ten thousand dollars. What else?" "That's all. That's all I have." "Nothing more?" "Well, I have a few dollars here in my pocket." "How much?" We start digging. "Well, let's see—thirty, forty, sixty, eighty, a hundred twenty dollars." "That's fine. What else do you have?" "Well nothing. That's all." "Where do you live?" He's still probing. "In my house. Yes, I have a house." "The house, too, then." He writes that down. "You mean I have to live in my camper?" "You have a camper? That, too. What else?" "I'll have to sleep in my car!" "You have a car?" "Two of them." "Both become mine—both cars. What else?" "Well, you already have my money, my house, my camper, my cars. What more do you want?" "Are you

alone in this world?" "No, I have a wife and two children. . . ." "Oh, yes, your wife and children, too. What else?" "I have nothing left! I am left alone now." Suddenly the seller exclaims, "Oh, I almost forgot! You yourself, too! Everything becomes mine —wife, children, house, money, cars, and you, too." Then he goes on. "Now, listen. I will allow you to use all these things for the time being. But don't forget that they are mine, just as you are. And whenever I need any of them you must give them up, because I am now the owner."

That's how it is, my friend. That's what it means to follow Christ.

THREE QUALIFICATIONS FOR DISCIPLESHIP

What qualities did these twelve men show that caused Jesus to call them? Why did Jesus ask them to follow him? The answer is in Luke 5: 27–29, in a description of Matthew:

"And after that He went out, and noticed a tax-gatherer named Levi, [his other name was Matthew] sitting in the tax office, and He said to him, "Follow Me." And he left everything behind, and rose up and began to follow Him. And Levi gave a big reception for Him in his house; and there was a great crowd of tax-gatherers and other people who were reclining at table with them."

I want you to notice three qualities that Jesus looked for when he chose his disciples. First, Jesus would invest his time in men who were available. When he said, "Follow Me," they left everything and followed him. Matthew was available; he followed Jesus.

Second, these men had "heart"; they had an eagerness for Jesus which is more important than a lot of information or a lot of abilities. Luke 5: 29 says that Levi was so thrilled to be asked to be a follower of Jesus that he threw a big party to introduce Jesus to all his friends.

Third, these men were teachable. The disciples were "ignorant" men, according to the sophisticates of the day, but they didn't stay that way! They were eager to grow, and it is wonderful to see what the Holy Spirit can do in polishing a man who goes hard after the Lord. Peter, who started out catching fish for a living, in the end became a magnificent, scholarly preacher and author of two of the world's most polished, balanced, and lofty writings, the works of a true master.

But it is interesting to note whom Jesus did not choose to be part of the inner circle. Nicodemus loved Jesus very much, and so did Joseph of Arimathea. These two men of influence and worldly stature were going to be strategically very important later on in Jesus' life. But I think they must have been too enmeshed in this world's system—not loose enough, not free enough—to be one of the Twelve.

THE BLESSING OF DISCIPLESHIP

What an honor, what a privilege it was to be chosen to live by the side of the earthly Jesus, absorbing all that was humanly possible, and then after Jesus' departure, to spread it to the rest of the known world! It was a fantastic assignment, with huge eternal rewards. But these twelve were no less privileged than we are! Second Corinthians 5: 16 says, "Therefore from now on we recognize no man according to the flesh; even though we have known Christ according to the flesh, yet now know we Him thus no longer."

There was no benefit in the apostles passing along such information as the physical characteristics of Jesus. The gospel was the important message. We can know the Lord as intimately as they did by the enabling of the wonderful Holy Spirit given to be our teacher. It is also our privilege to be at Jesus' elbow, to be part of his "inner circle," to leave all to follow him, to give our lives to making him known.

Study Questions

Review the text as you answer these questions.

1. What was Jesus' strategy for reaching all those crowds of Acts 2 with his message?

2. Do you think the crowds always understood and were sympathetic to the existence of the Twelve? Why?

3. Every Christian is a potential disciple. How can you tell if you will really become one?

II

The last words of any man are very important and the person to whom he tells them is very important, also. Most of us do not have the opportunity to prearrange that particular situation. But Jesus, just before his ascension, did have such an opportunity. He was God the Son going back to heaven again; he could have gathered a multitude, as at the Sermon on the Mount. But he only gathered his disciples and said to them these words: "All authority has been given to Me in heaven and on earth. Go therefore and make disciples of all the nations, baptizing them in the name of the Father and the Son and the Holy Spirit, teaching them to observe all that I commanded you; and lo, I am with you always, even to the end of the age" (Matt. 28: 18–20).

He gathered his inner circle of disciples around him and said, "Now, you've seen the way I made you my disciples. I let you stay close to me and watch me do everything I did. You could ask questions and share my life at close range. And I sent you out to minister, too, so that you learned by doing. Now it's time for me to go. Now *you* turn around and go make disciples, teaching them everything that I have taught you. That's my plan for spreading the gospel over the world. It will be a slow, sometimes painful way so that the gospel won't be diluted, but it's the way people will truly understand my Word, as they see it deeply rooted into human lives."

Obedience to the Great Commission

And this is exactly what the disciples did. When Peter preached that magnificent sermon on the day of Pentecost, and the 120 believers were joined by 3,000 new Christians, what was their plan for integrating the new ones into the faith? Acts 2: 41–42 says, "So then, those who had received his word were baptized; and there were added that day about three thousand souls. And they were continually devoting themselves to the apostles' teaching and to fellowship, to the breaking of bread and to prayer."

The word *they* apparently refers to 3,120 people—the new and the old. And their new lifestyle had four components:

1. *The apostles' teaching.* That is what Jesus had said for them to do—to go make disciples and teach them everything they had learned from Jesus. At first the teaching was oral; later on they wrote it down into what became the New Testament. For us today the equivalent would be Bible study.

2. *Fellowship.* Simply being together—working together, playing together, rejoicing and weeping together—all the ways in which their lives could melt into one.

3. *The breaking of bread.* Some versions say "Communion." And I'm sure Jesus intended to include that ritual, but surely this phrase also meant just having meals together. Remember that these were real people who had to work for a living, clean their houses, and so on. As they were deeply involved in learning and fellowship they surely would get hungry and often say, "Let's not separate! Let's have a simple meal together and keep going."

4. *Prayer.* The word used here is the same word as in Acts 3: 1 when Peter and John went to the temple at the hour of "prayer," or actually, "the prayers." This was the stated time for temple worship.

So our present-day equivalent to these four components of lifestyle would be Bible study, fellowship, eating together including communion, and church services all of which are to involve old as well as new Christians.

A BRAND NEW LIFESTYLE

The results then were spectacular! Acts 2: 43–45 says there was a great sense of awe over them all, and they lovingly shared their possessions as well as everything else. Verse 46 tells how frequently this new lifestyle was carried on: "day by day." And it tells the two places where it happened: "in the temple," and "from house to house." The large groups came together in the temple. Small groups met in homes. Discipling took place in both places; new Christians were to-

gether with older ones learning how to worship and becoming
a part of the local body of Christ.

Was structured discipling really possible during this time?
Did it really happen? Well, the ratio of new Christians to old
was twenty-five to one, and I think it really happened. Maybe
each older believer had three groups of eight each in his home;
daily would mean he could have each group twice a week. Apparently these new converts were thoroughly absorbed: "And
day by day continuing with one mind in the temple, and
breaking bread from house to house, they were taking their
meals together with gladness and sincerity of heart, praising
God, and having favor with all the people" (Acts 2: 46–47).

It sounds as if they were having a lot of fun as it happened.
And it worked so well that "The Lord was adding to their
number day by day those who were being saved" (Acts 2: 48).
Soon there were five thousand more Christians!

We need to look very hard at the workings of the early
Church, in its ideal condition with the first bloom of the fullness of the Holy Spirit upon it. This condition didn't last
very long, because by the eighth chapter of Acts the Christians were scattered by persecution. They could never again
do what they could do under those ideal conditions, but only
what they had to do under circumstances less than the best.
But at the beginning of the Book of Acts we see the church
during the "spring rains" of the fullness of the Holy Spirit.
And if we are coming into the "latter rains" of revival at the
time the Lord comes again, that could explain why we have
never been so interested in going back to copy that simple,
hard, joyous lifestyle of the early church.

CHRIST'S ONLY AUTHENTIC LIFE PATTERN

Jesus commanded his disciples and all the rest of us to go
into all the world and make disciples, teaching them everything we've been taught about Jesus. So we're to make sure
our lifestyles are thoroughly Christian, and then gather new
ones to us continually, who will watch and learn and partici-

pate until they can be off on their own, also discipling. This is Christ's method. It's not *a* way, it's Christ's way. Sometimes when I'm called to speak to pastors as one of many speakers, I'm told, "You tell them what your way is." I say, "Look, it isn't *my* way, it isn't *a* way, it is Christ's way. The way is discipleship."

Christ's method for winning the world is not some frantic, overnight crash program. Christians continually fall into that trap. We think it should be a big Billy Graham Crusade that comes in and does it all. Now, thank God for Billy Graham and mass evangelism, but Jesus' normal method, while he did sometimes go to the masses, was to take a few men. He worked with a few, he built a few, and he worked his life into the few.

This process is sometimes painful; it is often slow; but it is the most effective way. Paul the apostle said to young Timothy, "The things which you have heard from me in the presence of many witnesses, these entrust to faithful men, who will be able to teach others also" (2 Tim. 2: 2).

GOD'S WAY DEMANDS NEW ACCOMMODATION

Remember that Jesus introduced his choosing of the Twelve with the teaching that old wineskins aren't good enough for new wine. Moving in deeply to the personal lives of other human beings, as Jesus was about to do with twelve men, is not always comfortable business. Longterm Christians who've "never done it that way before" are apt to think they'd rather just keep sitting in their pews listening to sermons, and not get so involved.

Peggy and Jim are a truly beautiful couple who have been in God's family since they were children. Raised in Christian homes, they met as kids in a Christian private school. The church has always been their "scene." But when we invited them into a group of four couples with us, they didn't hesitate a minute. They adjusted their lifestyles to be new wineskins, to hold the good new thing God was going to do for them. And what good things he's done! What spiritual victories we've

seen in their family! How we've rejoiced with them as they've
led others to Christ! Their thrills are our thrills, as their hurts
are our hurts. These two longtime Christians were ready for
new wine from the Lord in their lives.

Discipling God's Way to Spread His Word

The goal is to reproduce Jesus Christ in somebody else. This
is the greatest thing you can ever do. It's more important than
your vocation. It is the key work of the Christian. You invest
yourself in someone who invests himself in someone who will
invest himself in someone. That's the way the church grows.

You must never be the end of the line of God's grace and
gospel. The water of life is intended to flow through you. You
are to be a conduit. You are to be a pipeline to others. Jesus
put it this way: " 'He who believes in Me, as the Scripture
said, "From his innermost being shall flow rivers of living
water" ' " (John 7: 38).

Ask God to give you a few people who are teachable, who
are available, and who have heart. Some people's lives are too
involved. Some people have "hardening of the categories";
they just can't break loose. Love them, but don't waste your
time on them; look for "faithful men who will be able to teach
others also."

Then give yourself to those few. This command isn't just
for pastors or graduates of a Bible school. Anyone can do this.
You just gather around Jesus and share what you know. If all
you know is John 3: 16, have a neighbor in for coffee who
doesn't know John 3: 16, and tell him about it. Then if he
says, "Hey, this was great! Could we do it again next week?"
—you've got seven days to learn something new!

One Generation at a Time

My mother had five kids. She lived ninety years and had lots
of grandchildren and great grandchildren. By the time our
third child was born, my older brothers and sisters had many
children. I wrote mother, "It's a boy!" I got back the most

unenthusiastic letter you can imagine! It had two words that referred to the birth of this new child in our family—*More Ortlunds!* That's all!

Sometimes I would ask Mother, "How did you raise those five mean little kids?" We'd joke about the early days. But if I'd asked her, "Mother, how did you raise the seventeen grand-children and the multitudes of great grandchildren?" she would have said, "Now, wait a minute! Those are your kids, not mine. I took care of five, and that's it. No more!" She would have been right. It wouldn't be fair to expect my mother to raise her grandchildren and her great grandchildren.

And that principle is true spiritually. You are to have your own family. Then they will have their family, and then they will have their family. A problem with the church is that the pastor has tried to be everything for all generations and all times, and he's often been frustrated.

DISCIPLING GOES DEEP

My Christian friend, if you are not in a discipleship ministry, as I understand the Bible, you are saying "No" to Almighty God. In not passing on the faith, you are becoming the end of the line.

I am not talking about a "hit and run" program where we only say, "How are you? Good to see you." People who only do that are "Hi" Christians. They go through life without really knowing people. We need to know people in depth, and give them our lives in depth. Pray for, love, care for, and become accountable to the few people God gives you, and let them be accountable to you. Make something of your life by the grace of God together.

I cannot state how important this has been in my own personal life. I've been with many groups and with couples, and I've grown to understand what it means for very different people to be unified in Christ.

Some years ago, I met with a group of eight men. I gathered

them together, and I said, "I want you to give me your hearts, and I want you to help me to love me. I will love you. We will share God's Word together; we will bear each other's burdens; we will meet together once a week, and we will give ourselves to each other. We're going to grow together. We're going to try to be effective ministers of Christ together." The group discussed the idea for a while, because it was a big step to commit that amount of time each week.

Then one of the men said, "Look men, this is not a discussion time. This is an altar call. Are you willing?"

And they gave their hearts to me for a year and a half. It was very crucial. It enabled me to carry out the ministry God gave me. That group, along with many other men who have since shared their hearts with me in groups like that, changed my life. It was really important to me, and still is.

Recently three of us were having breakfast together and sharing Christ. One of the men said to us, "You know, the thing that bothers me about people in the church is that they think that what they do, how they live, whether or not they are faithful, whether they witness, whether they are obedient, whether they surrender is all optional! They want to live as they please and then have heaven and eternity." He said, "It isn't optional! We are disciples of Jesus Christ."

Yes, my friend, discipleship is God's way. It's not optional! Don't miss out on God's plan for the world and for you!

Study Questions

Review the text as you answer these questions.

1. What does it mean to be a disciple? What does it mean in your own personal life or what could it mean?

2. What are the four components crucial to a truly biblical lifestyle? What two kinds of Christians are to carry these out, side by side? Do you see this happening around you?

3. Why is the lifestyle of the early church important to us today?

4. Why is discipling the most efficient method for church growth?

5

Christ's Transfiguration and Your Transfiguration

Luke 9:28–36

I

Every springtime a family of raccoons finds its way to our backyard, and at meal times they wash their food in our swimming pool. The first time they came these funny, furry animals were an amazement to our son who at the same time was learning some wonderful truths in Sunday School. One night he prayed, "Dear Lord, thank you that worms turn into raccoons, and that raccoons turn into butterflies." Then, still with his eyes tightly shut, he shook his head and said, "Lord, I just don't see how they do it!"

The process of metamorphosis is truly an amazing thing, and that process is what we discover was happening to Jesus in Luke 9:28–36. The word *transfigured* (sometimes translated *transformed*) in the Greek is *metamorphoō*, from which we get our English word *metamorphosis*. What happened to Jesus Christ in the transfiguration is more mysterious and wonderful than most of us have dreamed.

At the Birmingham Keswick Convention in Alabama some time ago, I realized again how the oratory and imagery of Southern preachers always sweeps me off my feet. One of the people there said, "All the preaching of this week makes me feel like a tadpole who's spent all his life in a small puddle being released into the Pacific Ocean!" The transfiguration of Jesus Christ makes me feel that way.

THE TRANSFIGURATION WAS ON SCHEDULE

First, look with me at the crucial timing of the transfiguration. "And some eight days after these sayings . . . " (Luke 9: 28). What were the "sayings" that preceded the transfiguration of Jesus? Well, for instance, see verses 18–20: "And it came about that while He was praying alone, the disciples were with Him, and He questioned them, saying 'Who do the multitudes say that I am?' And they answered and said, 'John the Baptist; but others say, Elijah; and others, that one of the prophets of old has risen again.' And He said to them, 'But who do you say that I am?' And Peter answered and said, 'The Christ of God.'"

This statement was a great milestone. And it was about eight days after this statement that Jesus was transfigured.

Another saying that preceded the Transfiguration was that for the first time Jesus told his disciples that he would die and rise again. Of course this news was shocking to them. "The Son of Man must suffer many things, and be rejected by the elders and chief priests and scribes, and be killed, and be raised up on the third day" (Luke 9: 22).

Now, Mark's Gospel says that when Jesus predicted his death and resurrection, Peter took him aside and began to rebuke him. Can you imagine that? He began to rebuke the one who would soon sit on the great throne of judgment and rebuke whole nations and kingdoms and principalities and powers in heaven and on earth. Peter had no idea yet of God's purposes in the cross, but in his rebuke he was representing all the forces that had struggled for ages past to keep the Son of God from dying for the sins of the world. And Jesus "let him have it." He said, "Get thee behind Me, Satan!" He was saying, "Peter, you are doing the devil's work. You are being his mouthpiece, because the devil doesn't want me to go to the cross, either."

GRACE GREATER THAN SIN

The disciples had six to eight days to think over these say-ings. Then the three disciples were taken up into the moun-tain alone with Jesus. Do you notice that even after Jesus had so severely rebuked Peter, he nevertheless took him up into the mountain to be alone with him and to let him in on one of the most glorious events of all Jesus' earthly ministry? You know what that tells me? That tells me that Jesus had a plan for Peter. I believe he's got a plan for you, and even your care-less and foolish speech will not interfere with that plan. You'll get rebuked for it, but this doesn't mean that you're lost from God's plan. I'm thankful for that. God didn't give up on Peter. Jesus took him up to the high mountain of Transfiguration.

At prayer meeting we were sharing from Galatians about the warfare in the believer's life—the flesh lusting against the Spirit, and the struggles we go through as people, regarding sin in our lives. One of the men told us that God had taught him a great lesson one day. He said, "It was like a flash of truth. When I ask forgiveness for a sin, and I go out and com-mit that same sin again, I'm tempted to think that I'm through. God will not forgive me." But he said, "I was going through a time of despair like that when God gave me insight. God seemed to say, 'The worst sin against me is not believing that I will forgive that sin.'" He said, "I left that experience a new man!"

David confessed his tragic fall into sin with Bathsheba in Psalm 51. But then when he was assured of forgiveness he made new plans to serve God and said, "Then will I teach transgressors thy ways ... "

PRAYER: THE SEAT OF ACTION

As we look at the Scripture's account of this amazing hap-pening, how important the words are in verse 28, Jesus "went up to the mountain to pray." In fact, verse 29 says that he was transfigured "while He was praying."

Remember that from the Mount of Transfiguration on, Jesus would set his face steadily toward the Mount of Crucifixion, and there was much to be done between these two events. His disciples needed to be taught, needed to be encouraged. I'm sure he was praying about the needs of these men and the concerns he had for them. Understand this, my friend: it was while he was praying that the transfiguration happened, and much of their need was met in the middle of that prayer by the transfiguration.

You see, prayer is not something you do before you act. Prayer is the action itself in which God moves the world. If you are in need of great insight, if you see a need for a miracle in your community or in your work or in your family, *pray.* Prayer is the way God gets it done. John Wesley said, "I have so much to do that I must spend several hours in prayer before I am able to do it." Out of prayer came the Transfiguration.

THE GLORY OF CHRIST EXPOSED

Besides the crucial timing of the Transfiguration, there was the crucial nature of the Transfiguration. Luke 9: 29 says, "And while He was praying, the appearance of His face became different, and His clothing became white and gleaming." The Transfiguration was not a spotlight from heaven coming down in special focus upon Jesus Christ the Son. It was not a reflection on his face, as Moses experienced when he had spent time with the Father. Rather, the Transfiguration was the inner deity and the magnificence of Jesus bursting forth through his humility. Remember that the tabernacle of the Old Testament had above the Mercy Seat in the Holy of Holies the Shekinah Glory, the Presence of God. Looking on the tabernacle, one would see the various coverings, of goat, and badger, and other skins. It looked like a very ordinary, humble building. So our Lord Jesus Christ was humanity outside, but deity and glory—the Shekinah Glory, the Holy of Holies—inside. And in that one glorious incident in his earthly life, his majesty burst forth.

His face was different as the Scripture says. And even his clothing shone. The word *gleaming* in our text means that his clothes "pulsated with splendor." Picture that in your mind! Or *gleaming* could also be translated "flashing like lightning" or "glistening."

THE LIGHT MADE LIGHT

I remember hearing Dr. Wilbur Smith say, "The brilliant light emanated from the transfigured body of the Lord—an emanation from the Fountain of Light within."

Days before, Luke 9:27 tells us that Jesus had said, "I tell you truly, there are some of those standing here who shall not taste death until they see the kingdom of God." Friend, this is it: a brief look at the King in his kingdom. In the Transfiguration, we see what Christ was like in his heavenly preexistence.

What a fantastic spectacle! Don't laugh at Peter because he began to babble like an idiot, not knowing what he was saying. Who wouldn't? Why, John saw him and passed out, says Revelation. If we saw the glory of Jesus right now, we'd all be flat on our faces, and there might be a lot of heart attacks. Oh, the glory of his presence!

In the Transfiguration Peter, James and John got a preview of the King in his kingdom. Jesus said, "Peter, that's what's ahead after the cross. Don't you worry about the cross. This is what's going to come." So we see Christ in his Transfiguration: what he was before, and what he's going to be in the great glory to come.

A CROSSROAD EVENT

The Transfiguration marked an important point in Christ's ministry, too. G. Campbell Morgan says in *The Crises of the Christ:* "It was the crowning of the first part of his mission, that of realizing perfect life. Because of this crowning, he was now able to pass to the second part of his mission, that of atoning death. . . . Had not the life been perfect, the death would have been nothing more than the tragic end of an ordinary life."

Christ had lived his life without sin. He was the first man since Adam who had no need to die, for death is the result of sin. In a sense, ever since Adam, God had "looked for a man" who would be perfect before him, and now at last, such a one had come: the "last Adam," the fulfillment of all God had planned for man to be.

So Jesus, having lived his perfect human life, could have soared from the Mount of Transfiguration right on back to heaven. Angels would no doubt have received him in great glory. The power of that wonderful life would have made his entrance triumphant indeed.

But if he had done that, without dying for us, he would have gone to heaven alone. There would never have been any people in heaven! Those Old Testament saints who went there on virtue of what Christ would do for them on the cross, looking forward to his atoning work, would have had to leave and go to hell.

> *There was no other good enough*
> *To pay the price of sin;*
> *He only could unlock the gate*
> *Of heaven and let us in.*
> —Cecil F. Alexander
> "There Is a Green Hill Far Away"

COMPANIONS IN GLORY

Now notice the details of what happened in this remarkable event. "And behold, two men were talking with Him; and they were Moses and Elijah, who, appearing in glory, were speaking of His departure which He was to accomplish at Jerusalem" (Luke 9: 30–31).

These men were two representatives of the Old Testament— Moses representing the law, and Elijah representing the prophets. They were obviously alive and well, as are all those millions who have died "in the Lord" over the centuries; but here they are made visible to people on earth. They also seemed to represent two kinds of death. Moses had died a natural death, even though the circumstances were certainly unique. Elijah had gone soaring off into heaven without dying. It seems that they represent the two situations of God's people at the time of the second coming of Christ in his glory.

FOCUS OF INTEREST: GOD'S LAMB

They had one subject. Heaven talks about one thing! It's very interesting that they didn't talk about the old days when they were here on earth. They talked about his departure. They talked about his coming cross. We can't imagine what it must have been like in heaven as these representatives of all heaven talked about the cross. I'm sure they were listening intently. For all the Old Testament believers were saved by virtue of following the commandments of God to offer sacrifices and be obedient to God, because Jesus would come and be the fulfillment of those sacrifices. The lambs in the Old Testament were slain as pictures of *the* Lamb of God who would die on the cross and take away their sins. Hebrews 11:13 says, "These all died in faith, believing. . . ." Believing what? God had told them in the Old Testament to offer sacrifices, and God knew the Lamb slain from the foundation of the world, as the Scripture says, would fulfill and perfect all that they dreamed and longed for.

The Old Testament believers, then, sacrificed in obedience to God's command. This saved them in advance of the coming of Jesus Christ, the Lamb of God, who would take away the sins of all the world. Hebrews 10:12 tells us, "He, having offered one sacrifice for sins for *all* time. . . . " So you see, at the very middle of history is the cross. And all Old Testament people were saved by the cross. It was the great redemptive blow of God for every one of us. "On Him was laid the iniquity of us *all*" (Isa. 53:6). This perfect, transfigured Christ was slain for us. So Moses and Elijah were very interested, on behalf of all heaven, to talk about his departure which he would accomplish at Jerusalem. It was very important.

A CLIMACTIC EXODUS

Notice that they called Christ's death his "exodus." That word *departure* means "exodus." No one could talk about an exodus like Moses! He had led the children of Israel out of the land of tyranny and bondage, out of Egypt where they were outside the will of God and in sin. Moses was the one to redeem them out of Egypt. God used him as the great leader for that situation.

Now the great exodus for all time was approaching—the exodus that was going to take place at Calvary. Jesus would lead all his redeemed ones "out of the pit," out of sin, out of suffering, out of death, into his triumph and righteousness and acceptance with the Father, and into eternal life.

The first "exodus" had been accompanied by the Passover experience, when a lamb was slain and his blood shed to redeem the families of Israel. Now Jesus' "departure" would make him the Lamb "slain before the foundation of the world," for the sins of all.

The first "exodus" had also been accompanied by the crossing of the Red Sea. And now, at the cross of Christ, God would open a way for us to cross over right into the presence of the Father, into the Land of Promise forever.

This exodus was more than his death. It was Christ's resurrection, also, and his ascension to heaven. It was a full exodus. It's important for us to see the meaning of this, because this is Jesus that we're talking about, the Savior on whom we are placing all our hope, my friend. Look at this! Heaven talks about Jesus. They talk about his cross in heaven. The subject is "Worthy is the Lamb that was slain, to receive glory and honor. . . . " Heaven sings about Jesus and his cross.

TRYING TO BE HELPFUL

Now, Peter makes a suggestion in the midst of the talking of these two representative saints of the Old Testament. He says this: "Let's make three tabernacles." A tabernacle was a brush lean-to. I don't know what these men would have done with a brush lean-to! It's humorous to think about. Peter was so nervous, so overcome by all of this that he just began to jabber. Luke says he didn't realize what he was saying. But while he was talking, " . . . A cloud formed and began to over-shadow them; and they were afraid as they entered the cloud. And a voice came out of the cloud, saying, 'This is My Son, My Chosen One; listen to Him!' " (Luke 9: 34–35). Moses and Elijah faded away. As it says in the other Gospels, "They saw no man save Jesus only."

The disciples went down in silence. They couldn't say any-thing. But I believe this was a turning point. They could never be the same again. They had seen the glory of Jesus.

A SECRET LATER DISCLOSED

Peter, James, and John were the only three disciples allowed to view this wonderful event. The Gospels of Matthew and Mark tell how Jesus gave them orders not to relate to anyone what they had seen, "until the Son of Man should rise from the dead" (Mark 9: 9). I'm sure all three were bursting to tell it!

James never wrote any permanent Scripture (the epistle of James was written by a different James.) But the other two disciples wrote of this experience; how could they not write of it? John wrote, "And the Word became flesh, and dwelt among us, and we beheld His glory, glory as of the Only Be-gotten from the Father, full of grace and truth" (John 1: 14) .

Peter wrote, "For we did not follow cleverly devised tales when we made known to you the power and coming of our Lord Jesus Christ, but we were eyewitnesses of His majesty. For when He received honor and glory from God the Father, such an utterance as this was made to Him by the Majestic Glory, 'This is My beloved Son with whom I am well pleased,' and we ourselves heard this utterance made from heaven when we were with Him on the holy mountain. And so we have the prophetic word made more sure, to which you do well to pay attention as to a lamp shining in a dark place, until the day dawns and the morning star arises in your hearts" (2 Pet. 1: 16–19).

Study Questions

Review the text as you answer these questions.

1. Describe in your own words what the transformation may have looked like.

2. What relationship does the Transfiguration have to history and to eternity, both before and after?

3. How might the Transfiguration have contained the seeds of temptation for Jesus?

4. Compare the exodus of the children of Israel with the exodus of all believers through the cross.

II

When the three disciples were taken up the mountain and there saw Jesus metamorphosed before them, they were absolutely awestruck. And so should we be, to discover that the very same Greek word is used in 2 Corinthians 3: 18 to describe what God does to us: "But we all, with unveiled face beholding as in a mirror the glory of the Lord, are being transformed into the same image from glory to glory, just as from the Lord, the Spirit."

This concept is so amazing, so wonderful, we need to examine it more carefully and find out exactly what process God is using to make us finally like himself.

There are two Greek words which have been translated various ways interchangeably in the New Testament: one is *morphē* and the other is *schēma*. Both are sometimes rendered "transform," sometimes "transfigure," sometimes in newer versions "change" or "disguise." We need to separate the two and find out what they're actually telling us.

The word *morphē*, as we have said, means to transform in a way so that what the person genuinely is, is allowed to emerge and be seen. So on the Mount of Transfiguration (or Transformation) God simply allowed to be exposed what Jesus truly was. There was no spotlight coming down from heaven to make him "look glorious." His inner reality, with all its magnificence, came bursting forth through his humility.

Wonder of wonders, the same word *morphē* is used by the Holy Spirit to say that we believers are in the same process of being transformed, or transfigured. What we truly are by God's grace—our genuine inner reality—is emerging more and more through our outward lives, as we keep our eyes fixed on Jesus and allow it to happen.

ANOTHER KIND OF OUTWARD CHANGE

The second Greek word, *schēma*, means only to appear to change when you really are not changed on the inside, like putting on a mask. This word is used three times in 2 Corinthians 11: 13–15: "For such men are false apostles, deceitful workers, disguising themselves as apostles of Christ. And no wonder, for even Satan disguises himself as an angel of light. Therefore it is not surprising if his servants also disguise themselves as servants of righteousness; whose end shall be according to their deeds."

Satan sets the example: he "is transformed," as the King James Version says. His followers copy him, "transforming themselves," putting on their masks and pretending to be what they're not.

That's why the whole idea of Christians coming to church "with masks on," or as we say, with smiling faces to hide the real person inside, doesn't make any sense. When we wear masks we are acting like the devil, for one of two reasons. Either we don't realize who we truly are, that God has made us new and put his glory within us, therefore we hide, not realizing what we hide. Or else, we are not taking time to see Christ in his Word, and we become weak and fearful, so we try to hide from our brothers. Either way, we're in bad shape, and the wrong needs to be righted.

PAUL'S EXPOSÉ OF HIMSELF

In 2 Corinthians 2: 17, Paul is stunned that the Corinthian Christians had misread him, and he says, "For we are not like many, peddling the Word of God, but as from sincerity, but as from God, we speak in Christ in the sight of God."

The next section through 2 Corinthians 4: 15 deals with Paul's ministry, his discipling, his relationships with his spiritual followers. "You Corinthians," he says, "are the very letter of recommendation for my life!" (How would you grade your life, my friend, judged by the quality of your disciples?) He sums up the passage saying again that he is open and sincere before them, that he speaks only what he believes and only for their sakes (2 Cor. 4: 13–15).

In the meanwhile, he's not strutting! Oh, I know what it is

to start to get puffed up and to feel God's gentle hand on me putting me back down again. There's this interesting dichotomy here, that we are to be sincerely open with people and that as we are open, glory will be exposed; and yet at the same time it's all of Christ and none of us. And that fact gives us a genuinely healthy self-image! Notice Paul's word: "Not that we are adequate in ourselves to consider anything as coming from ourselves, but our adequacy is from God. . . . " (2 Cor. 3: 5) . "But we have this treasure in earthen vessels, that the surpassing greatness of the power may be of God and not from ourselves; we are afflicted in every way, but not crushed; perplexed, but not despairing; persecuted, but not forsaken; struck down, but not destroyed; always carrying about in the body the dying of Jesus, that the life of Jesus also may be manifest in our body" (2 Cor. 4: 7–10).

The way the glory of Christ emerges from us in continual transfiguration is for our old self to be continually put to death. Transfiguration is all bound up with identifying with Christ in both his death and his resurrection. "For we who live are constantly being delivered over to death for Jesus' sake, that the life of Jesus also may be manifested in our mortal flesh" (2 Cor. 4: 11). And that's the secret to living, the secret to openness in discipling, the secret to living the life of continual transformation.

AN UNFADING GLORY

Now, we've gone all the way around 2 Corinthians 3: 18 to get the context of it, so let's go back and take another look at the actual verse. Paul has been leading up to it by saying that Moses' experience of glory was *not* a continual thing; he had to keep trying to hide his face with a veil so that *his* public wouldn't notice that the glory was fading. But in the new administration of God's wonderful grace, says Paul, we can openly and continually display God's glory with no fear of fading: "But we all, with unveiled face beholding as in a mirror the glory of the Lord, are being transformed into the same image from glory to glory, just as from the Lord, the Spirit" (2 Cor. 3: 18).

This mirror does what no earthly mirror can do: it changes the one who looks! And it's a continuous process of "ever-increasing splendor," as one Christian put it. It's like Proverbs 4: 18: "But the path of the righteous is like the light of dawn, That shines brighter and brighter until the full day." The pilgrimage of the Christian isn't "from the log cabin to the White House," or "from rags to riches;" it's "from glory to glory!" It starts with glory, and it ends in more glory! "Therefore," says Paul, "since we have this ministry, . . . we do not lose heart." (2 Cor. 4: 1).

God is so encouraging! His path for us is sometimes hard, but still it is glory all the way, increasing glory. That's his principle, forever: the best wine is last; the New Covenant is better than the Old; heaven follows earth. Praise the Lord!

WITHIN CHRISTIANS: GLORY

And Paul says, since we have this ministry of openness, before all our spiritual followers, knowing that God is at work in transformation, causing increasing glory to emerge, "We have renounced the things hidden because of shame, not walking in craftiness or adulterating the word of God, but by the manifestation of truth commending ourselves to every man's conscience in the sight of God" (2 Cor. 4: 2) .

There's not a single Christian who doesn't need to get hold of this truth! Those who clutch to themselves their privacy in shyness and inhibition need to see it. Pastors, missionaries, all who don't want to live openly because they're protecting their "image" need to see it. Those who are dogged by the guilt of past sins need to see it—that all has been forgiven, and so as they look to Jesus and open up in ministry, glory will be revealed, not their old sins!

Adam and Eve, in their sinless perfection, were naked before each other and were not ashamed. They had nothing to hide! We need to realize how completely forgiven we are, and

that we can learn to be transparent with each other because
there is nothing to hide! Our sins have all been washed away,
and there is only increasing glory to be revealed.

DISPLAYING THAT GLORY

I know that many Christians for instance, have never been
willing to be in small groups because they don't believe in
"confession sessions," and they're "afraid of airing dirty linen."
I don't blame them; I feel the same way. I have no desire for
anybody to know what some of the past sins in my life have
been. But that is Satan's false view of what small groups are
all about, to instill fear in believers and keep them from being
obedient to a biblical lifestyle. Jesus said, "Where two or
three are gathered together in My Name, there am I in their
midst" (Matt. 18: 20). His presence is so cleansing, so purify-
ing, so uplifting!

I've gathered with small groups in the name of Jesus for
many years, and I've never seen or heard anything revealed in
poor taste. Our eyes are on him. Sometimes, after we know
each other well, a sin may be confessed, in order that we may
pray for that one so that he may be healed, as James 5: 16 says
will happen. But it's wonderful to be healed of a sin! How
much better than keeping it bottled up inside where it festers
and hurts! My brothers and sisters in Christ in these loving
"pockets of shalom" have never done me anything but good.

Discipling takes openness. Like Paul, we must be "sincere,"
showing how the word of God has worked itself out in our
particular lives, being real with them, so that they can learn
to be real with us.

My friend, the transfiguration in our lives takes place just
as it did in Jesus': it is "from the Lord," and it is before our
dear ones, our spiritual followers.

Second Corinthians 3: 18 says that transfiguration is a process God is doing within us. What a comfort! But Romans 12: 2
says it's also a command: "Be transformed [same word,
morphē] by the renewing of your mind. . . . "

Let's cooperate in the process God is carrying out!

Study Questions

Review the text as you answer these questions.

1. How is the process of metamorphosis, which results in a visible outward change, different from putting on a mask and costume? (Compare Christ's experience with ours, which uses the same Greek word.)

2. Christians who hide their inner selves don't understand what is inside. What is?

3. Describe all you know of the Apostle Paul from what he exposed of himself in his writing.

4. When small groups gather around the Lord, what will govern what is appropriate to say and what is not appropriate?

5. Is our transfiguration something we do or something God does?

6

Christ's Death
and Your Death

Luke 23: 32–49

I

A group of us were in Jerusalem at the Eastern Gate, the gate through which Jesus rode into Jerusalem that Palm Sunday. We were having a wonderful time, as we remembered that not only had Jesus come through that gate in past days, but he would come through again in great glory, according to Zechariah, at his second coming to earth. We began to sing quietly a hymn of praise. As we sang, guards from the Mosque Omar on the temple site began to storm down on us, furious at what they thought was Christian prayer on their sacred Moslem grounds. We got just a little bit of the feeling of what the early church experienced in hostility, the strange sensation of going from adoration to being caught suddenly in an emotional battle of persecution.

Jesus entered Jerusalem in all the praise of that first Palm Sunday, but soon he was to go through trial and be crucified.

What do you suppose would have been the result if Jesus had only ridden gloriously into Jerusalem, and then not died for our sins? Encyclopedias might read this way: "Jesus, born in the Jewish year of 5411 of humble Jewish parentage. He claimed to be the expected Messiah of the Jewish people. He lived to old age. The doctrines which he preached never took root among mankind. He died in obscurity."

But the word *cross* comes from the Latin word *crux*. And truly the cross is the crux of everything.

The Cross Through All of History

The cross was the crux of the Old Testament. What was the meaning of that event on Mount Moriah, when a trembling father raised his knife to slay his only son, if it was not Jesus' cross? What was the meaning of the serpent of brass, lifted up for healing, if it was not the cross of Jesus, where he was lifted up? What was the meaning of the Paschal Lamb, if it was not the cross of Jesus? Who was the suffering one of Isaiah 53, "wounded for our transgressions," if it was not Jesus at the cross? Who was the Kinsman Redeemer, if it was not Jesus, made like us, redeeming us? Who was Zechariah's suffering one, who was the stricken shepherd, if not Jesus, the good Shepherd who died for his sheep?

The Old Testament led up with a great crescendo to the cross of Jesus. The New Testament has as its very center the cross of Jesus. It's the crux of the New Testament. After the transfiguration, Luke says, Jesus "resolutely set His face to go to Jerusalem" (Luke 9: 51), to the cross. Paul, after preaching in the great intellectual center of Corinth, wrote back to the people there saying, "I determined to know nothing among you except Jesus Christ, and Him crucified" (1 Cor. 2: 2). And to the Galatians he wrote, "May it never be that I should boast, except in the cross of our Lord Jesus Christ, through which the world has been crucified to me, and I to the world" (Gal. 6: 14).

The whole Bible is from start to finish the Book of the Cross. The cross is the crux of everything. Someone said it this way: "To understand the cross is to understand the Bible. Conversely, to stumble over the cross is to find the Scriptures a mass of riddles. It's like reading a Shakespeare play and missing the plot."

Now let's study the actual story of the crucifixion of Jesus found in Luke chapter 23.

THE CROSS: THE CRUX OF INDIVIDUAL LIVES

Two groups of people illustrate coming to the cross—the crossroads—where they make decisions about Jesus. There were the criminals being crucified alongside Jesus. And there were the soldiers and their captain, who put them there: the robbers and the cops, you might say.

The two criminals were just that, but in several versions of the Bible they are called thieves, robbers, malefactors. Luke 23: 32: "And two others also, who were criminals, were being led away to be put to death with Him. And when they came to the place called The Skull, there they crucified Him and the criminals, one on the right and the other on the left."

A LESSON TO THE PUBLIC

Both of these men were certain of immediate death, death for crimes that they had committed. You see, it's one thing to die, but it's another thing to die as a criminal. And they were dying in a public place. The Skull was a hill by a busy thoroughfare, so that people passing by would get the message. Rome was saying, "Look, if you don't cooperate, this is what will happen to you."

In Jerusalem on a Sunday morning, I walked toward what is called "Gordon's Calvary." The famous Gordon thought that this particular site is the infamous Place of the Skull. It is an awesome place, a hill whose cavelike indentations mark out the eyes, nose, and mouth of a human skull. And as you come away from the hill there is a tomb which possibly could have been Jesus' tomb. As I stood there all alone that Sunday morning, I turned to my right and watched the Jerusalem bus terminal, busy, horns blaring, and people going in all directions. I thought about Jesus, crucified on a hill like that with the two criminals, and people jeering at them, wagging their heads as they went by.

INDIVIDUAL MEN, INDIVIDUAL RESPONSES

These two thieves each made a response to Jesus. "One of the criminals who were hanged there was hurling abuse at Him, saying, "Are You not the Christ? Save Yourself and us!" (Luke 23: 39).

Here was a man who had lived an ugly life and was dying an ugly death. And out of his mouth comes Satan's own temptation of Jesus in the wilderness, three years before. Satan had said, "You don't need to go to the cross. Let me show you a short-cut." Here was a last-ditch temptation again: "Save Yourself and get down!"

But, you see, if Jesus had saved himself, he could not have saved us. Then he would have missed the whole point of his coming into the world: "Thou shalt call his name JESUS: for he shall save his people from their sins" (Matt. 1: 21, KJV). Jesus resisted his temptation, and this man went to hell, cursing Christ all the way.

But the second criminal became a believer. In the last hour of his life he turned to God! "But the other answered, and rebuking him said, 'Do you not even fear God, since you are under the same sentence of condemnation? And we indeed justly, for we are receiving what we deserve for our deeds; but this Man has done nothing wrong.' And he was saying, 'Jesus, remember me when You come in Your kingdom!' And He said to Him, 'Truly I say to you, today you shall be with Me in Paradise'" (Luke 23: 40–43).

This man saw two basic, essential truths. He admitted his own sinfulness, and he admitted that Jesus was not a sinner. And even today, when a person comes to Christ with a willing heart and an open mind, the Holy Spirit peels back the ignorance and pours in the truth of God. The "eyes of your heart" can be enlightened.

THE MOST CRUCIAL REQUEST OF ALL

Then this criminal asked Jesus the all-important question. Verse 42 says that "he was saying. . . ." Evidently he was repeating, "Jesus, Jesus, remember me, Jesus, when You come in Your kingdom. Jesus, remember me!" He had lived a criminal life, and he was about to die, and he said, "I want to go to heaven!" That is not audacity; that is faith. We are all more or less in his position.

John Calvin made a wonderful comment about this man's faith: "How clear was the vision of the eyes which could thus see in death, life; in ruin, majesty; in shame, glory; in defeat, victory; in slavery, royalty. I question if ever since the world began has there been so bright an example of faith."

And Jesus said to him, "Truly I say to you, today you shall be with Me in Paradise." *Paradise* is the Greek word for *garden*. In Genesis 1 to 3, a garden was man's God-given dwelling-place. In Revelation 2: 7 it's the same: man's God-given dwelling-place, in other words, heaven.

Death has lots of mysteries, but here we see that this thief who repented would be in heaven before the day was out, as soon as he died. I like what one person said in regard to that passage: "We have one account of a death-bed repentance in order that no man need despair; we have only one, in order that no man may presume."

So here are two criminals at the crossroads. They died having chosen different directions. They hung there in the same spot, the "Place of the Skull"—but only briefly. Then they separated one hundred and eighty degrees.

THE MILITARY FACING DECISION

There were also soldiers and their captain at the crossroads. "And when they came to the place called The Skull, there they crucified Him and the criminals. . . . But Jesus was saying, 'Father, forgive them; for they do not know what they are doing.' And they cast lots, dividing up His garments among themselves" (Luke 23: 33).

These brutal men, probably four from what the history books tell us, were assigned to the crucifixions. The centurion, or their captain, was over the group. Time went slowly, so they gambled for his clothing. They did anything to pass the time. Luke says that they mocked him, saying, "Where are your cup bearers, O King? How about a drink?" and they offered him their cheap wine.

Again, they also asked the devil's question: "If You are the King of the Jews, save Yourself" (Luke 23: 37). They appealed to his pride: "You look so helpless up there. We heard you were somebody who had power!"

Apparently the struggle to keep Jesus from dying that sacrificial death was very real. In the Garden of Gethsemane Jesus had prayed, perspiring drops of blood in his agony, "Father, don't let me die prematurely." I believe that's what his prayer meant. "Let this cup pass from Me. I don't want to die before I go to the cross. Save me from dying too soon."

The warfare of the universe was raging as Jesus bore that wooden cross to Calvary and was hung on it; but up to the very last moment the temptation was still there, in the mouths of the soldiers, "Avoid it, Jesus!"

But he prayed for them. Perhaps he was praying for everyone. But it seems to me that his prayer was particularly for the soldiers nailing him to the cross and mocking him and gambling for his clothes. I'm sure he was praying for more, but surely his prayer included these.

JESUS' STRONG INTERCESSION

He did not say "Father, forgive me"; He said, "Father, forgive them." He did not die for his own sins; he died for our sins—all of our sins. He did not pray, "Father, bless them; help them; use them." He prayed, "Father, forgive them." Their great need was for forgiveness; without that, they would have no hope.

This does not mean that they were instantly forgiven; it means that they were potentially forgiven. There is a doctrine called universalism which says that when Jesus died on the cross, everyone was forgiven—they just don't know it yet; when they get to the Judgment Day they will discover that they're all saved.

But the Scripture points out over and over in many ways that we each have a responsibility to accept what Christ has done. There is his part, but there is also our part. The Bible says that "God was in Christ, reconciling the world to Himself, not counting their trespasses against them" (2 Cor. 5: 19). But the same Bible, in the very same passage, goes on to plead, "Be reconciled to God" (v. 20).

Understand this clearly in your mind. God has nothing against us. All our sins have been paid for. Jesus did indeed die for the world, but now the world has to say yes back to Jesus. Reconciliation is not completed until it involves both parties. So the Bible plainly says, "Believe on the Lord Jesus Christ, and thou shalt be saved." These men were all potentially saved. Christ did his part; but now they must do theirs.

Probably some of those who were around the cross at that time were also listening to Peter as he was preaching in Acts 3: 17 and 19. Peter said to them, "And now, brethren, I know that you acted in ignorance, just as your rulers did also. . . . Repent therefore and return, that your sins may be wiped away, in order that times of refreshing may come from the presence of the Lord." You see, their part was to repent and return, the response of belief and faith. Forgiveness is not automatic, but it is there for everyone.

He Became Sin for Us

You may feel that there is something in your background that you can hardly even think about, let alone tell anyone else about. There is forgiveness for that, absolute forgiveness. You can be utterly free. "Jesus paid it all."

"Father, forgive them"—the kindest, most needed words in all the Bible. Now quiet your heart a minute. I want you to listen deep, deep down inside. Listen to this. Hear it in your soul. "Father, forgive them. Condemn *Me*." That's what He was saying. "Forgive them, condemn Me"—the just for the unjust. Jesus took our place.

The prayer was answered. How many have been forgiven? The thief was forgiven right away and brought to heaven. Then there were the three thousand at Pentecost, then the five thousand after that. All through the ages there have been the millions of people who have been forgiven. And I've been forgiven. Praise God! Christ died for all of us.

Are you forgiven? You see, when you come to the cross, you come to a crossroads. You cannot go in the middle. There is no middle ground. You're either forgiven, or you bear your own sins. Jesus wants to forgive you, wants to absolutely cleanse you.

The last we hear of the soldiers are those words in Luke 23: 37: "If You are the King of the Jews, save Yourself!" What a terrible way to go into the future!

WHEN NATURE MOURNED

Before we look at their captain, notice verses 44 and 45: "And it was now about the sixth hour, and darkness fell over the whole land until the ninth hour, the sun being obscured. . . ."

The phrase *the whole land* here is not the Greek word for the inhabited earth, meaning the Roman Empire and other areas where people lived. This is normally translated "world." Certainly it's not the territory of Judea. The Greek word means the physical earth, the planet, with the adjective *whole* added to make the sense very clear.

Verse 45 says that the sun was obscured, or literally, "failed." The Greek word *fail* is our English word *eclipse;* but it could not have been a natural eclipse because at Passover time the moon was practically full, and on the opposite side of the earth from the sun.

So this was an unnatural darkness, a mystery mentioned by Matthew, Mark, and Luke, with no attempt at explanation.

We know that creation is affected by sin. In Genesis 3: 17–18 as a result of Adam's sin the earth was cursed and would from then on bear thorns and thistles and be hard to get a living

from. Romans 8 continues the story: "For all creation is waiting patiently and hopefully for that future day when God will
resurrect his children. For on that day thorns and thistles,
sin, death, and decay—the things that overcame the world
against its will at God's command—will all disappear, and the
world around us will share in the glorious freedom from sin
which God's children enjoy. For we know that even the things
of nature, like animals and plants, suffer in sickness and death
as they await this great event" (Rom. 8: 19–22, LB).

Joel says that great wonders in the sky will accompany the
Lord's final judgment of the earth—the sun turning to darkness and the moon to blood, and so on. And here at the crucifixion, nature called the "Firstborn of all creation," and this
event shared more with creation than we understand.

THE DEEPEST AFFLICTION

God drew the curtain of darkness so that none could see
those last three hours of Jesus' suffering, bearing our sins at
the cross. The Bible never goes into the gory details of his
death, and probably we should not either. It was blotted out
by this obscuring or eclipse, this supernatural or unnatural
darkness. In the daylight, the Lord suffered at the hands of
men; but in the darkness, he suffered the judgment of God. In
the daylight was the injustice of men; but in the darkness came
the full wrath and the justice of God. In the daylight, man
hated the Sin-bearer; but in the darkness, God poured out his
judgment on the sin. That's why the truth of that old hymn
"There Were Ninety and Nine" is so important for us to know
and to remember:

> None of the ransomed ever knew
> How deep was the valley crossed;
> Or how dark was the night
> That the Lord passed through
> Ere He found the sheep that was lost.
> —Elizabeth C. Clephane
> "The Ninety and Nine"

THE RIPPING OF THE VEIL

And then Luke 23: 45 also says that the veil of the temple was torn in two: simple words with enormous meanings behind them! The temple in Jerusalem through the centuries had been the symbol of God's presence. And particularly, the most precious part of the temple was a room called the "Holy of Holies," where for a long time the Shekinah Glory was: a glorious light which was God's actual presence. By Ezekiel's time, more than half a millenium earlier, Israel had become so wicked that the Glory departed. But the Holy of Holies was still the symbolic place of God.

In front of it was an enormously thick, heavy veil. The historian Josephus says it was eighty feet high, twenty-four feet wide, and several inches thick. The Old Testament describes it as totally covered with embroidery in red, blue, and purple.

Matthew 27: 51 says that at the actual moment of Christ's death, the temple veil was torn right in two from top to bottom. No man could have done it; it was an act of God. And Hebrews 10: 19–20 describes why God tore it: "And so, dear brothers, now we may walk right into the very Holy of Holies where God is, because of the blood of Jesus. This is the fresh, new, life-giving way which Christ has opened up for us by tearing the curtain—his human body—to let us into the holy presence of God" (LB).

JESUS' SPIRIT DISMISSED

Then continuing with Luke 23: 46, "And Jesus, crying out with a loud voice, said, 'Father, into Thy hands I commit My spirit.' And having said this, He breathed His last."

There is so much mystery here! Don't ever feel you have this story figured out. It will take all eternity, I think, for us to get the full ramifications. But now Jesus has drunk the last dregs of the cup of bitterness, and he says, "Into Thy hands I commit My spirit." Everything had worked up to that moment. And now we read in the other Gospels that there was an earthquake, tombs were opened and dead men walked out, and so on! It was as though a symphony orchestra, playing a great composition, had built to a mighty climax with tympani and cymbals crashing and clashing together. It was as though God was using all nature to give his great "Amen! Nothing deterred him! Victory! It's done!"

At this point, when the centurion saw what had happened, he began praising God. That seems like an odd response unless we undersand that the deepest meaning of praise isn't necessarily joyous. God gave the centurion insight to see that "certainly this Man was righteous;" and from the depths of his being, the one who was in charge of the execution bowed down in awe and acknowledgement that this was no less than the Son of God (Matt. 27: 54). Faith and eternal life came to that man at that moment.

THE CROSS, THE DIVIDER OF MEN

Like the criminals and like the soldiers, every person who lives comes to the crossroad of the cross. After the execution these soldiers probably walked down the hill together, but they were not together. One walked one way, and the other went the other. That is, the troops apparently went one way, and their leader went the other. There are really only two kinds of people: those who believe in Christ and those who don't. The cross makes the difference.

A man and his wife may live all their adult life together, but one may go one way into eternity, and the other will go the other. The same might be true of a father and son. How they love each other! Dad often has his hand on his son's shoulder, affectionately saying by that gesture, "Son, I love you." But if the son loves Jesus and the father doesn't, they are an eternity apart. Each person must make his own decision.

The crux of everything is the cross. Sin was dealt with at the cross: "Father, forgive them," Jesus said. Heaven was opened at the cross: "Today you will be with Me in Paradise." All the evidence was in, at the cross: "Truly, this was the righteous One."

In London, on the sidewalk just outside Wesley Chapel, is a large statue of the great preacher and hymn writer, Charles Wesley. He is standing in his clergy robe with his arms outstretched, and he is still preaching, as it were, to the people on the sidewalk. Underneath the statue of this earnest preacher are these words: Oh, let me commend my Saviour to you!

At the crossroads, the will of God is that you simply give one of these responses: "Lord Jesus, remember me. . . . Certainly you are the Righteous One." Accept the forgiveness and entrance into heaven that Jesus makes available to you!

Study Questions

Review the text as you answer these questions.

1. Describe the difference between the effect of Christ's death on Old Testament believers and on New Testament believers.

2. When God looked down on three crosses, on which heads did he place the blame for sin?

3. What do we learn about the Christian's life after death from what Jesus said to the repentant thief?

4. Are all sinners automatically forgiven as Jesus requested, because "they know not what they do"? Explain your answer.

5. "The Jews require a sign" (1 Corinthians 1: 22). What visual signs proved that Christ's death was of special significance?

6. Why does Jesus' death affect each human being personally? How have you responded to his death?

II

"Christ died for my sins": that's the gospel to the unbeliever. "I died with Christ": that's the gospel to the believer.

Once you accept Jesus Christ by faith and cross over into God's family, a whole new truth begins to become wonderfully clear. You discover that personal, spiritual dying brings practical living!

As we have said, the cross of Christ is the crux of the world's history. And it's also true that your own personal cross is the crux of your personal history as a Christian.

OUR DEATH, HIS DEATH

Let us look at Galatians 2: 20: "I have been crucified with Christ; and it is no longer I who live, but Christ lives in me; and the life which I now live in the flesh I live by faith in the Son of God, who loved me, and delivered Himself up for me."

Some false religions merely *use* the cross, for their own purposes; but the cross does not permit accommodation. Verses like this one in Galatians are so strong, they cannot be tampered with. Wycliffe's old English translation of this verse said, "I am fixed to the cross!" I am lashed there; I am nailed there; I cannot get down!

It is crucially important for you to see that you have been crucified with Christ, that what happened to him also happened to me and to you; that what he went through to pay for sin, *God credits to your account.*

Here is total identification, like the paper in the book. *I am in Christ,* and I *have been* (past tense) crucified with Christ. Now I must reckon it to be so.

There is sin, which is the root; and there are sins, which are the fruit—the result of sin. The cross goes deep to deal with the root of sin. Christ's salvation is not a fire escape! He comes to change you deeply, where you truly need it. And he does it not by schemes of self-improvement, but by crucifixion. Oh, how we need to hear this today!

When Adam sinned, he died as a result. Death became our inherited condition. No child was ever born good, he wasn't even born neutral! This is why letting our children "express themselves" is simply letting out that old sinful nature. Permissiveness just exposes the true human heart, in all its need for God and for redemption.

THROUGH DEATH, NEW LIFE BEGINS

But though Adam's fall was a deadly fall, Christ's glorious death and resulting resurrected life is even more powerful. The "second Adam," Christ, God's new man, would be the progenitor of a new family—a family of the cross! New beginnings are so wonderful. The first Adam started a corrupt family, but the second Adam began again in total power and victory for us all. God illustrated it once this way; when he said to the prophet Jeremiah, "Go down to the shop where clay pots and jars are made and I will talk to you there. I did as he told me and found a potter working at his wheel. But the jar that he was forming didn't turn out as he wished, so he kneaded it into a lump and started again. Then the Lord said: O Israel, can't I do to you as this potter has done to his clay?" (Jer. 18: 2–6, LB).

Through the cross and the resurrection of Christ, God makes a brand new person. The old you—so touchy, so weak, so vulgar—is dead, really dead. But we need to "reckon it to be so," as Romans 6: 11 tells us to do. Are you living as a crucified person? Here's the way Paul expressed it: "As for me, God forbid that I should boast about anything except the cross of our Lord Jesus Christ. Because of that cross my interest in all the attractive things of the world was killed long ago, and the world's interest in me is also long dead" (Gal. 6: 14, LB).

CONSIDER YOUR DEATH TO BE TRUE

During times of temptation it's especially important to *reckon* yourself to be dead to sin—to count it to be so.

A man has been a life-long alcoholic. What's the one thing

that will cure him? "Jesus Christ," you say. Yes, but suppose
he never accepts Christ? There is one thing which will absolutely cure him of his thirst for alcohol: death. When that
man dies, you could wheel his casket right by his favorite bar;
he won't respond. You could pass a bottle of whiskey right
under his nose; he won't care. Death will cure him completely
of his weakness.

"Even so, consider yourselves to be dead to sin, but alive to
God in Christ Jesus" (Rom. 6: 11). Or as the Living Bible
says, "So look upon your old sin nature as dead and unre-
sponsive to sin, and instead be alive to God, alert to Him,
through Jesus Christ our Lord." When I reckon sin to be dead
in me because of God's Word, God sees my faith, and works
on my behalf.

Galatians 2: 20 is an intensely personal verse. Notice how it
is peppered with "I's" and "me's": "I have been crucified with
Christ; and it is no longer I who live, but Christ lives in me;
and the life which I now live in the flesh I live by faith in the
Son of God, who loved me, and delivered Himself up for me."

INDIVIDUALLY PRECIOUS

Self-crucifixion certainly doesn't mean self-negation. God
isn't trying to obliterate me as an individual.

Recently I was in Bolivia, and out in the jungle at night, the
Milky Way seemed like a glamorous, broad sash that belted
the whole sky. But I know God doesn't see it just as a sash; he
knows each individual star. In that same way Gal. 2: 20 makes
us very much individuals. We're not just part of a mass!

Are you still fearing the thought of the crucifixion of self as
if you were going to lose out on some fun or some real "good-
ies" in this world? There was a time when Elijah stretched
himself out on a dead child—hands on hands, feet on feet,
mouth on mouth—and the child became alive again. So when
the cross is laid over me, though before I was dead, I become
warm and alive and exhilarated and empowered. "I have been
crucified with Christ. . . . I now live. . . ."

The *I* which died was an overbearing master. The *I* which lives is a contributing, loving servant. The *I* which died loved to be ministered to. The *I* which lives loves to minister!

The *I* which died was a source. The *I* which lives is a channel.

NEW LIFE, NEW POWER

And this life which I now live—in contrast to my life before Christ—is still in the flesh, but no longer living after the flesh, or in the weakness of the flesh. I have the same tongue; but before it cursed, and now it blesses. I'm still "in the flesh," but the crucifixion of self has changed all that. Otherwise, remaining in the flesh, with the new things that we know as God's children, would be unbearable! "Wretched man that I am! Who will set me free from the body of this death? Thanks be to God through Jesus Christ our Lord!" (Rom. 7: 24–25).

BIBLICAL "SELF-IMAGE"

This truth is in direct contradiction to the false "wind of doctrine" blowing around these days which says "Love yourself." If you examine the Scriptures carefully, you will never find once that God commands us to love ourselves. Several times he assumes that we naturally do love ourselves and tells us to go far past that to the important loves of neighbor and wife.

But clearly understand the strong, tough, hard, beautiful message that God wants us to hear about ourselves: "Jesus said, . . . 'If anyone wishes to come after Me, let him deny himself, and take up his cross, and follow Me. For whoever wishes to save his life shall lose it; but whoever loses his life for My sake shall find it'" (Matt. 16: 24–25). "And he who does not take his cross and follow after Me is not worthy of Me" (Matt. 10: 38). "If anyone comes to Me, and does not hate his own father and mother and wife and children and brothers and sisters, yes, and even his own life, he cannot be My disciple. Whoever does not carry his own cross and come after

Me cannot be My disciple" (Luke 14: 26–27). "Do you not
know that all of us who have been baptized into Christ Jesus
have been baptized into His death? Therefore we have been
buried with Him through baptism into death, in order that
as Christ was raised from the dead through the glory of the
Father, so we too might walk in newness of life. For if we have
become united with Him in the likeness of His death, certainly we shall be also in the likeness of His resurrection,
knowing this, that our old self was crucified with Him, that
our body of sin might be done away with, that we should no
longer be slaves to sin; for he who has died is freed from sin"
(Rom. 6: 3–7). "Now those who belong to Christ Jesus have
crucified the flesh with its passions and desires" (Gal. 5: 24).

DIE TO SELF, LIVE TO GOD

See yourself as lashed to the cross! Believe it by faith! Then
the flesh becomes only faith's *instrument,* to be used for God's
glory. Live by faith. Work by faith. Rest by faith. Play by
faith. Faith is *working energy.* Martin Luther said: "Faith
connects you so intimately with Christ that the two of you
become one person. As such, you may boldly say, 'I am one
with Christ.' You may say, 'His righteousness is mine.' And
Christ says, 'His sin is Mine. I am willing to be totally joined
to him into one flesh.'"

Dietrich Bonhoeffer, who suffered for his faith in a German
prison, wrote strong words which are the mirrored side to
Jesus' words to us, "Go, and live!" Bonhoeffer's words are
these: "When Christ calls a man, he bids him come and die."

Study Questions

Review the text as you answer these questions.

1. What plan did God devise to dig the very most of sin out of our lives?

2. What will be our attitude toward ourselves as we live crucified lives? Toward Christ?

3. Does counting ourselves as dead mean our mind-set will be morbid and gloomy? Why or why not?

7

Christ's Resurrection and Your Resurrection

Luke 24: 1–48

I

We thank God for Christmas—a time that is precious to us all. But Jesus is not in the manger. We give thanks to our Lord for the earthly life of Christ. He showed us how to live, but he no longer walks the hills of Galilee. And we do give thanks for the very serious and comforting day called Good Friday, but Jesus is no longer on the cross or in the tomb.

We give praise for Easter. Christ lives! In a real way, it's Easter on Christmas. For Easter is not an event that passes, but continues. It happened, and the effect goes on and on. In a sense, Christmas is really Easter Day. Good Friday is really Easter Day. If Easter is in your heart, today for you is Easter Day.

Vance Havner, a well-known evangelist, was asked to go to the Holy Land. "No," he said, "I don't want to go." "Why?" he was asked. He answered, "I don't want to go where Jesus *was;* I just want to stay right where Jesus *is!*"

THE FIRST EASTER

Let's look at the twenty-fourth chapter of Luke, starting with the first verse: "But on the first day of the week, at early dawn, they came to the tomb, bringing the spices which they had prepared. And they found the stone rolled away from the tomb, but when they entered, they did not find the body of the Lord Jesus. And it happened that while they were perplexed about this, behold, two men suddenly stood near them in dazzling apparel; and as the women were terrified and bowed their faces to the ground, the men said to them, 'Why do you seek the living One among the dead? He is not here, but He has risen. Remember how He spoke to you while He was still in Galilee, saying that the Son of Man must be delivered into the hands of sinful men, and be crucified, and the third day rise again.' And they remembered His words, and returned from the tomb and reported all these things to the eleven and to all the rest."

Continuing from verse 44, "[Jesus] said to them, 'These are My words which I spoke to you while I was still with you, that all things which are written about Me in the Law of Moses, and the Prophets and the Psalms must be fulfilled.' Then He opened their minds to understand the Scriptures, and He said to them, 'Thus it is written, that the Christ should suffer and rise again from the dead the third day; and that repentance for forgiveness of sins should be proclaimed in His name to all the nations—beginning from Jerusalem. You are witnesses of these things.' "

SEE THE RESURRECTION WITH NEW EYES

The resurrection is really the climax of the earthly life and ministry of Jesus. First of all, Scripture tells us that it is the climax of everything Jesus himself taught as he was with his disciples. His teachings all funneled into Easter morning. The angels, or the messengers of God, said that Jesus' earlier words to his disciples had really explained everything!

I wonder how many things we look at, but really don't see. Or how much we hear, but don't listen to. One day I was sitting on our couch and reading the evening paper. My little boy was chattering away to me, asking me questions, and I was mumbling, "Yeah, uh-huh, yeah. . . . " He was getting very frustrated with me. Finally he reached around the paper, took my face in his two hands, and said, "Daddy, look me in the nose!" He wanted my attention, and he got it!

All heaven had been listening to Christ, but the earthlings to whom he had been speaking didn't understand him. In fact, just after Jesus had driven the moneychangers out of the temple and had performed his first miracle, changing the water into wine, John 2 says, " 'What right have you to order them out?' the Jewish leaders demanded. 'If you have this authority from God, show us a miracle to prove it.' 'All right,' Jesus replied, 'this is the miracle I will do for you: Destroy this sanctuary and in three days I will raise it up!' 'What!' they exclaimed. 'It took forty-six years to build this Temple, and you can do it in three days?' But by 'this sanctuary' he meant his body. After he came back to life again, the disciples remembered his saying this and realized that what he had quoted from the Scriptures really did refer to him, and had all come true!" (John 2: 18–22, LB).

The angels had heard this, and they understood it. So at the tomb the angels said, "Don't you remember this?" There was a little barb in their words, as the women came with the spices to anoint the body of Jesus: "Don't you remember what He said? What are you doing with those spices, anyway? What do you need those for? You are seeking the living in a place where dead people are."

ANGELS GOT IT; MEN DIDN'T

All heaven clearly understood it. Christ had laid out his plan that he would die and that he would rise again. Luke 9: 22 says, "The Son of Man must suffer many things, and be rejected by the elders and chief priests and scribes, and be killed, and be raised up on the third day."

Later Jesus got even more specific: "And He took the twelve aside and said to them, 'Behold, we are going up to Jerusalem, and all things which are written through the prophets about the Son of Man will be accomplished. For He will be delivered up to the Gentiles, and will be mocked and mistreated and spit upon, and after they have scourged Him, they will kill Him; and the third day He will rise again' " (Luke 18: 31–33). And then these strange words: "And they understood none of these things, and this saying was hidden from them, and they did not comprehend the things that were said" (Luke 18: 34).

But though they didn't understand, the resurrection is the gathering point of all the teachings of Christ. Everything he taught, said, and did, was to focus on the resurrection. That was the big victory, the big event!

Christ was made sin for us at the cross; he took our guilt upon himself. And God turned his back on his Son, with all the pain that must have caused. Nevertheless he did it, and Christ bore our sins, going down into death for us. If that isn't true, there isn't any hope for you and for me. Because, then, God, to vindicate his Son and verify that he had thoroughly paid for our sins, raised him out of the grave, and made him victorious over all that defeats man.

The gospel, you see, doesn't explain Easter. Easter explains the gospel. Christ was God. The miracle wasn't that Christ rose from the dead. It would have been even more unthinkable for the God/Man who was born as he was, and lived as he did, and died as he did, *not* to rise from the dead!

UNDERSTAND THE RESURRECTION

Don't let Christ's words about his death and resurrection, about the Easter event, become kind of "god-talk" that you simply tolerate because it's religious, with your tongue in your cheek a little bit. Friend, it's the only hope you have. These women came to the tomb with spices, and they hadn't the slightest idea that Jesus would rise from the dead. All the disciples believed the doctrine about the resurrection, in a "theological" way. If someone would have said, "Do you believe in the resurrection of the dead?" they would have answered, "Oh, sure—way off in the future sometime." It went into their mental files under a section labeled "Theology not important now." All the time they were thinking, I suppose, that these were some of his hidden sayings and parables. It must have absolutely blown their minds when they found out that Jesus really did rise from the dead, that he was not speaking symbolically or poetically, but that he meant precisely what he said.

CRISIS OPENS OUR EYES

Christ had said that the cross was inevitable and also that the resurrection was inevitable. Sometimes we hear things so often that the full meaning goes right past us. Perhaps the circumstances aren't right. It seems that we've got to hurt a little bit to open up to Jesus. It seems rare that the person who is on top with everything going his way cries to the Savior.

I remember when I was a young teenager, I had heard the Easter message and the gospel many, many times. But then a time came when I really heard and listened to it. Things weren't always smooth sailing from then on, but there was a new power and a new person. I was being made new. I became a Christian and began to grow. It was like a new life.

You may also have had that experience. It's a glorious thing. Because then when you really are ready to hear, God gives you instant recall, as he did that first Easter: "[Then] they remembered His words, and returned from the tomb and reported all these things to the eleven and to all the rest" (Luke 24: 8). Then they remembered his words. They were ready. And after they had heard, they were ready to tell.

THE EARLIER WRITINGS FORETOLD IT

Not only did Jesus' words predict his rising from the dead, but the entire Old Testament points to and focuses on that event as well! The resurrected Christ sat and ate broiled fish with his disciples and said to them, "These are My words which I spoke to you while I was still with you, that all things which are written about Me in the Law of Moses and the Prophets and the Psalms must be fulfilled" (Luke 24: 44).

"Then He opened their minds to understand the Scriptures, and He said to them, 'Thus it is written, that the Christ should suffer and rise again from the dead the third day; and that repentance for forgiveness of sins should be proclaimed in His name to all the nations—beginning from Jerusalem.'" (Luke 24: 45–47).

My family and I love to visit the beautiful Albert Memorial Chapel in London. Along the sides of the chapel are marvelous carvings of the Old Testament prophets. Each one is so distinct—Isaiah, Jeremiah, Jonah, and others. But they are all doing the same thing: holding out their arms and pointing their fingers forward toward the altar of the church. And at the altar is a huge sculpture of the empty tomb, the stone rolled away, and Jesus coming out of that tomb, full of life, strength and vitality, smiling as though he were saying, "All hail! Hello!" The prophets are all pointing to the risen Christ.

PROPHECY IN MANY GARMENTS

The Old Testament portrays the resurrection in a number of different ways. We see a beautiful example of Christ's resurrection in the willingness of Abraham to offer up his "only begotten son" on the altar of sacrifice, and yet doing it in strong resurrection faith, saying to the servants, "Afterward I and the lad will . . . come again to you" (Gen. 22: 5). Listen to the way Hebrews 11: 19 (Living Bible) explains Abraham's thinking: "He believed that if Isaac died God would bring him back to life again; and that is just about what happened, for as far as Abraham was concerned, Isaac was doomed to death, but he came back again alive!"

In actual words, probably even older than Abraham, is the clear text of Job: "As for me, I know that my Redeemer lives, and at the last He will take His stand on the earth. Even after my skin is flayed, yet without my flesh I shall see God; Whom I myself shall behold, and Whom my eyes shall see and not another" (Job 19: 25–27). Have you ever heard a more forceful description of the resurrected Christ?

THE NEW TESTAMENT'S USE OF THE OLD

The essence of Peter's blood-and-thunder sermon on the day of Pentecost was that the Old Testament prophecy provided proof of Jesus' resurrection. "God raised Him up again, putting an end to the agony of death, since it was impossible for Him to be held in its power. For David says of Him, 'I was always beholding the Lord in my presence; for He is at my right hand, that I may not be shaken. Therefore my heart was glad and my tongue exulted; moreover my flesh also will abide in hope; because Thou wilt not abandon My soul to Hades, nor allow Thy Holy One to undergo decay . . . '" (Acts 2: 24–27).

And Peter goes on to say that David wasn't writing about himself, because he certainly died and they all knew where his tomb was, but, "He looked ahead and spoke of the resurrection of the Christ, that He was neither abandoned to Hades, nor did His flesh suffer decay . . . " (Acts 2: 31).

It would have been wonderful to listen to the newly risen Jesus open up the Old Testament to his disciples to show how his death and resurrection were taught there. Earlier the same day he had spent time teaching two people on the road to Emmaus the same thing: how Moses and the prophets showed that Christ must suffer and then enter into his glory. And it made their hearts burn within them!

Norval Geldenhuys in *The New International Commentary: The Gospel of Luke* sums it up for us: "And through the centuries there are untold multitudes, the poor and the rich, the simple and the educated, the aged and the young, millions who day after day experience in their own hearts and lives the assurance that Jesus has indeed risen and that he lives as Lord and King. In the testimony of the Holy Ghost in the heart of every reborn child of God no doubt exists, and together with the believers of all ages our hearts sing":

He lives! He lives!
Christ Jesus lives today!
He walks with me and talks with me
Along life's narrow way.
He lives! He lives!
Salvation to impart:
You ask me how I know He lives?
He lives—within my heart!
                    —Alfred H. Ackley
                    "He Lives"

Study Questions

Review the text as you answer these questions.

1. Angels understood the resurrection (verses 5–7) but they don't understand everything (1 Peter 1: 12). What seems to be the role of angels in important events? See Luke 1: 11, 19–20; 26–28; 2: 8–11.

2. Why is the truth of the resurrection so important to each of us personally?

3. Show at least two places where the New Testament proves that the Old Testament predicted Jesus' resurrection.

4. Show at least two of these predictions in the Old Testament. Rejoice over the miraculous, sure Word of God!

II

Two fellows had to make an emergency trip across an enormous lake. They simply had to do it! As they raced for the water's edge it was beginning to get very dark and they knew they'd have to make the trip in the night. They climbed into a boat there and began to row. A chilling wind came up. The waves got higher and splashed over the sides, drenching them continually. Their arms and backs ached with fatigue, but still they kept on rowing through the night.

At last there were a few faint signs of the coming dawn, and through the dimness they could see the approaching shore. Then, as it became more light, they looked around in their little boat and to their amazement discovered that in the back there was a motor! They hadn't even been aware of it! If they'd only realized it was there, they could have sped across that lake in comparative comfort and ease!

Every child of God is on his way to heaven, and it's true that now "we see darkly," but then, "face to face." But God tells us over and over in his Word that he gives us resurrection power to make the trip. Many Christians aren't aware of it, and they struggle on their own power through the dark night of this life, aching and miserable all the way. Their destination will still be heaven, and I suppose when they get there and learn of the unused power that was available to them, they'll say, "You gotta be kidding!" Perhaps that's what some of the initial tears will be all about.

BEGIN TO UNDERSTAND HIS POWER

But the Apostle Paul revealed God's longing heart when he wrote, "I pray that you will begin to understand how incredibly great his power is to help those who believe Him. It is that same mighty power that raised Christ from the dead and seated him in the place of honor at God's right hand in heaven, far, far above any other king or ruler or dictator or leader. Yes, his honor is far more glorious than that of anyone else either in this world or in the world to come. And God has put all things under his feet and made him the supreme Head of the church—which is his body, filled with himself, the Author and Giver of everything everywhere" (Eph. 1: 19–23, LB).

Think of the power of a plant, pushing out of a little seed to struggle up through darkness and very heavy dirt, alone and unaided, and to push its way up into the world, even if it has to crack cement sidewalks to do it.

Think of the power of a small bundle of sticks of dynamite —just a small bundle—suddenly transformed into so much power that it can blast apart a whole mountain side and pave the way for super highways.

Think of the power of a rocket, no higher than a several-story building, which can be made to shove so hard against the side of the earth that it can crash through all the pull of gravity and soar out into the universe's unknown space.

Now think of the power of *God,* to take a broken, dead body in a dusty little tomb in the Middle East some two thousand years ago, breathe back into it the eternal life of his own Son; roll stones away; lift it from a spot near Bethany, up through this atmosphere and all known heavens, through hosts of spiritual enemies and even out of time to his own right hand, the place of authority and blessing and power forever and forever! *This* is the power given to you, if you are a believer!

PRACTICAL POWER FOR TODAY

Now maybe you're saying, "Well, I just can't comprehend it; it doesn't mean anything to me." Let's picture one of our pioneer forefathers out in his fields in western America. Suppose we could go to him and say, "Guess what! You have the potential to fly! In a hundred years you'll be taking off in jet planes and even rockets to the moon!" I think he'd look sort of puzzled and scratch his head and say, "Yes? Well, that's just dandy, but I don't see how that power is going to help me plow my corn any better. . . ."

Likewise what we must understand is that the knowledge

God longs for us to have is not that *some day* we'll be resurrected; that's not enough to help us today. So the Holy Spirit goes on to explain to us that this is our *past and present* experience: "God, being rich in mercy, because of His great love with which He loved us, even when we were dead in our transgressions. . . ." (Eph. 2: 4, 5a).

We were as spiritually impotent as that limp body lying in an ancient Middle Eastern tomb; we had no spiritual life. And for those of us in that condition, he did three things: ". . . Made us alive together with Christ, and raised us up with Him, and seated us with Him in the heavenly places, in Christ Jesus, in order that in ages to come He might show the surpassing riches of His grace in kindness toward us in Christ Jesus" (Eph. 2: 5–6).

Notice here our identification with Christ. If you can believe it happened to him, you can believe it has happened also to you.

LET YOUR MIND TAKE HOLD OF IT

You mean that we're there now, together with Christ? Yes. It's mysterious; it's even mystic. But in the spiritual realm, in learning to understand God's Word, seeing is not believing; believing is seeing. First, if God says it, you count it so. Then you begin to understand it.

And when you begin to live every day believing that the old "you" was crucified and that you've been made alive together with Christ, you begin to understand the "greatness of His power toward us who believe" (Eph. 1: 18).

Romans 6: 11–13 tells us to count it to be so: "Even so consider yourselves to be dead to sin, but alive to God in Christ Jesus. Therefore do not let sin reign in your mortal body that you should obey its lusts, and do not go on presenting the members of your body to sin as instruments of unrighteousness; but present yourselves to God as those alive from the dead, and your members as instruments of righteousness to God."

For the Christian, this concept inspires a whole new mentality.

INVISIBLE INNER STRENGTH

Here's a glove. When I hold it up, it just dangles down; it's totally impotent. It is useless. But suppose I put my hand into it. "Oh," people begin to say, "What a powerful glove! What dexterity it has! It can do anything!" You and I are totally weak, my Christian friend, in ourselves. But when we begin to realize the power that has come into our lives, available at our disposal, and when we begin to use it, people may start to say, "What a powerful Christian! He's fantastic!" But you and I will know the power is not from; it is God's resurrection power within us.

"But if the Spirit of Him who raised Jesus from the dead dwells in you, He who raised Christ Jesus from the dead will also give life [energy, power; one translation says vivaciousness] to your mortal bodies through His Spirit who indwells you. So then, brethren, we are under obligation, not to the flesh, to live according to the flesh—for if you are living according to the flesh, you must die; but if by the Spirit you are putting to death the deeds of the body, you will live" (Rom. 8: 11–13).

CHRIST'S RESURRECTION AND YOURS

Let's turn back to our resurrection text in Luke 24 and get a picture of inner resurrection power.

Early Easter morning, women came to the tomb. (In verse 1, *they* refers to the women of Luke 23: 55, 56.) Verse 10 tells *what* women: Mary Magdalene, Mary the mother of James, and Joanna.

Verses 2 and 3 describe their shock: the stone was rolled away, and the body of Jesus was gone. Verses 4 and 5 tell of their terror: two strange, glittering men were there instead.

Verses 6 to 8 explain *why* the shock and terror: they were without the Word of God in their hearts; their insides were a vacuum; they were living "from the outside in," and so upsetting circumstances crushed them like eggshells.

Verse 8 is pivotal: "Then they remembered His words." Prompted by the angels, the Word of God sprang to life within them, and then they were fearless: they began running, telling, and even directing the disciples to go to Galilee (Mark 16)!

And now it's up to you. Will you let the Word of God spring to life within you, that Word that has described to you God's resurrection power for you? If you are a Christian, *you have that power.* The Holy Spirit is within you, and he is utterly sufficient for you to be everything spiritual you ever dreamed of being. He can cause you to live the risen life—every moment of every day!

> *Soar we now where Christ has led, Alleluia!*
> *Following our exalted Head: Alleluia!*
> *Made like Him, like Him we rise: Alleluia!*
> *Ours the cross, the grave, the skies. Alleluia!*
> —Charles Wesley
> "Christ the Lord
> Is Risen Today"

Study Questions

Review the text as you answer these questions.

1. What practical difference does it make for a Christian to understand his own spiritual resurrection?
2. Think of God's power described throughout the Bible. (Use a concordance if you like.) Why is resurrection power a great gift to the believer?

3. Which is the strongest part of a Christian: the invisible

inside or the visible outside? This should give us new appreciation for each one.

4. What part does the Word of God play in the way we view ourselves, and therefore the way we function?

8

Christ's Ascension
and Your Ascension

Luke 24:50–53
Acts 1:1–11

I

In South America, on the border of Argentina and Brazil, are the Iguassu Falls. They are so large that they are like a whole string of Niagara Falls. My wife and I explored this phenomenal sight after ministering in Bolivia. We were tired and desperately needed the refreshing experience we had there. For about an hour we walked along the opposite bank of those falls. As we rounded a turn there burst out before us the scene of glorious, unimaginably large, billowing falls. We walked on, and at another turn in the path there were more falls, then more and then more until we were just stunned with the beauty.

As you read and study the three short years of the ministry of our Lord Jesus Christ, you come upon one grand and glorious vision of him, one holy view of him, one unimaginably beautiful scene of him here, there, here, there, until you are stunned with the power and dignity of Jesus Christ.

LUKE'S ACCOUNT OF THE ASCENSION

This last view of Christ on earth is truly spectacular. Luke doesn't say much about Jesus' ascension as he closes his Gospel, because he plans to write another book in which he will give more attention to that event. In this Gospel he writes only, "And He led them out as far as Bethany, and He lifted up His hands and blessed them. And it came about that while He was blessing them, He parted from them. And they returned to Jerusalem with great joy, and were continually in the temple, praising God." (Luke 24: 50–53).

That last phrase actually carries history all the way to Acts chapter 8. But as we go back and begin the Book of Acts, Luke's second book, we get the details of Jesus' last appearance: "The first account I composed, Theophilus, about all that Jesus began to do and teach, until the day when He was taken up, after He had by the Holy Spirit given orders to the apostles whom He had chosen. To these He also presented Himself alive, after His suffering, by many convincing proofs, appearing to them over a period of forty days, and speaking of the things concerning the kingdom of God. And gathering them together, He commanded them not to leave Jerusalem, but to wait for what the Father had promised, 'Which,' He said, 'you heard of from Me; for John baptized with water, but you shall be baptized with the Holy Spirit not many days from now.' And so when they had come together, they were asking Him, saying, 'Lord, is it at this time You are restoring the kingdom to Israel?' He said to them, 'It is not for you to know times or epochs which the Father has fixed by His own authority; but you shall receive power when the Holy Spirit has come upon you; and you shall be My witnesses both in Jerusalem, and in all Judea and Samaria, and even to the remotest part of the earth.' And after He had said these things, He was lifted up while they were looking on, and a cloud received Him out of their sight. And as they were gazing intently into the sky while He was departing, behold, two men in white clothing stood beside them; and they also said, 'Men of Galilee, why do you stand looking into the sky? This Jesus, who has been taken up from you into heaven, will come in just the same way as you have watched Him go into heaven.' Then they returned to Jerusalem from the mount called Olivet, which is near Jerusalem, a Sabbath day's journey away" (Acts 1: 1–12).

Under the most accessible part of the Iguassu Falls, we stood wide-eyed and thrilled to watch the cascading water tumbling down, indescribably large and beautiful. Right beneath the falls was a glass souvenier shop, wet from the sprays. In the midst of all this glory, the girl at the counter sat utterly bored. This experience was an everyday occurrence for her.

We come to the ascension of Jesus. We've read about it many times. We must never let it be "old stuff" to us.

I see in this event two hooks on which we are going to anchor our thoughts. The first is that the ascension of Christ completed his earthly ministry. The second is that the ascension commenced his heavenly ministry. Now, think with me about these two doctrinal truths.

THE FINAL GLORIOUS CHORD

The ascension of Jesus Christ from this planet to heaven was the "amen" to his earthly life. And it was a logical amen. The factual, historical writer Luke had already indicated that Christ's resurrection was unquestionably settled and established by his disciples. By that I mean that they were satisfied that he had indeed risen from the grave, because he had met them in the mountains and by the sea, in a room and on the path. And by twos and fours and by sevens and by twelve and by one hundred twenty and now also five hundred, it was settled.

Acts 1: 3 says, "He also presented Himself alive, after His suffering, by many convincing proofs, appearing to them over a period of forty days."

Now, the last appearance. Luke tells us when it happened, where it happened, how it happened, and what was said at the time. We have all that information right here. Where did it happen? In his Gospel, Luke said it wasn't far from Bethany. The Book of Acts says the Mount of Olives. In either case it was just a Sabbath day's journey from Jerusalem.

What was said? All the recorded conversation is here.

When did it happen? Forty days after his resurrection, in broad daylight with everyone who was there looking on.

So we read in verse 9: "After He had said these things, He was lifted up while they were looking on, and a cloud received Him out of their sight." This event was logical. It would not have been logical for the appearances to go on and on and on, and then finally peter out to nothing. Certainly Jesus was not going to die again after his resurrection.

Into Another Sphere

And it says a cloud received him out of their sight. In the Scriptures the cloud is often the visible, physical symbol of the presence and glory of God. Here, it would seem, the Shekinah Glory of God was receiving his son. We also remember in the Book of Daniel the Son of Man riding upon the clouds of heaven to be crowned with glory by God (Dan. 7: 13). Christ left his disciples and went back to the presence of the Father and the glory of heaven.

We are creatures of time and space, and it's hard for us to comprehend eternity and heaven. Someone put it this way: "He 'ascended on high' is not a phrase meant to signify a position further above sea level, but rather to a higher sphere of existence."

We must not get too hung up on the word *up*. What difference does it make whether we say he went up or beyond or away or over? Perhaps the preposition should be *out*, because he broke out of earth and into heaven, out of time and into eternity. One day he will break back in again, as the angels said! So we see that his ascension was a logical conclusion to his stay on earth.

Described in Advance

The ascension was also a prophesied conclusion. It was predicted in the Psalms of the Old Testament, and it was predicted in Jesus' own statements in the New Testament. The Psalms particularly gave many previews. Psalm 110: 1: "The Lord says to my Lord, 'Sit at My right hand Until I make Thine enemies a footstool for Thy feet.'" Peter and Paul reading this by the inspiration of the Holy Spirit said that these were the words of the Father installing the Son back into the glory and the primacy of heaven again (Acts 2: 34–35 and Heb. 10: 12–13).

Another psalm, Psalm 68: 18: "Thou hast ascended on high, Thou has led captive Thy captives."

Psalm 24: 9–10: "Lift up your heads, O gates, And lift them up, O ancient doors, That the King of glory may come in! Who is the King of glory? The Lord of hosts, He is the King of glory."

This last psalm is a preview of the ascension of Jesus Christ. It described the scene in heaven. If all the angels sang and praised when Jesus came at the incarnation at Bethlehem, and they did, what must have been the praise in heaven when Jesus returned again in glory and power? It must have been a wonderful, magnificent, musical event. Revelation 5: 9–14 hints at this fact when it says that they saw the Lamb upon the throne, seated in heaven, glorified, ascended, magnified there. All the angels, all the creatures of heaven called upon all the earth to sing praises to God. They said, "Worthy is the Lamb that was slain to receive power and riches and wisdom and might and honor and glory and blessing. . . ."

They joyously celebrated when they welcomed Jesus Christ back to heaven again.

And Jesus himself, before his death and resurrection, prophesied his ascension. He said, "Does [my difficult statement] cause you to stumble? What then if you should behold the Son of Man ascending where He was before?" (John 6: 62). And after his resurrection he said to Mary Magdalene, "I ascend to My Father and your Father, and My God and your God" (John 20: 17).

The ascension of Christ was a logical conclusion to his

earthly sojourn; it was a prophesied conclusion; and it was a satisfying conclusion. It was not threatening to his disciples. At his resurrection they had been afraid, but after his many appearances to them as the risen Christ, as they saw him ascend to heaven again they were thrilled! They knew they could not possibly lose on this one. His ascension was great gain to them.

HANDS IN BENEDICTION

I love the way Jesus is pictured as leaving. His hands are outstretched, and he is blessing them.

Dr. Wilbur Smith, teacher of the Koinonia Sunday School Class of Lake Avenue Congregational Church, once said, "These holy hands of our Lord, now seen for the last time, had once been employed in the carpenter's shop of Nazareth, for making a living for Mary and her fatherless children; these hands had lifted up the fallen, held little children, touched the leper, opened the eyes of the blind, had broken bread in the feeding of the five thousand, and the four thousand, had held a whip in driving out the money changers from the temple, had distributed the elements at the last supper, were cruelly pierced with nails on the cross, had been employed in making a fire on the shore of Galilee after the resurrection; and here are extended in an attitude of grace and benediction, as He parts from those who had been with Him for the last three years."

One of the dear fathers of our church congregation was just about to go off into eternity, and he gathered his whole family around his bed—his wife, his three sons and their wives, and his grandchildren—and raised his hand and pronounced the Aaronic Benediction: "The Lord bless you, and keep you; The Lord make His face shine on you, And be gracious to you; The Lord lift up His countenance on you, And give you peace" (Num. 6: 24–26). And with that, he died. What a way to go!

It was the way Jesus went. In the Jewish ritual, when the high priest finished the sacrifice, he lifted his hands in blessing as he dismissed the people. Jesus had finished his sacrifice. He had ended his earthly ministry and was about to begin his heavenly ministry. So he ascended to heaven, with arms outstretched, blessing his people. How warming, filling, and satisfying for those eleven men!

BACK TO HIS GLORY

And so his ascension was a great hinge. It was the end of the old, and the beginning of a new life for him—full of authority, seated at the right hand of the Father. The throne is now occupied by the one for whom it was made, the Lamb of God who took away the sin of the world. In heaven he is the authority; on earth he is the authority. Jesus said in his Great Commission, "All authority is given to Me in heaven and in earth. Go therefore. . . ." In heaven he is authority because all the hosts asked, "Who is this King of glory?" The answer was, "The Lord of hosts, the Lord mighty in battle, He is the King of glory." Where is glory? It's certainly in heaven. He is the King of glory, established on his throne in the heavens, he who rules the heavens.

He is the King upon earth. He's come to be authority on earth. It's his authority under which we operate. They said to him in Acts 1: 6–7: " 'Lord, is it at this time You are restoring the kingdom to Israel?' He said to them, 'It is not for you to know times or epochs which the Father has fixed by His own authority.' "

He did not deny the fact that the kingdom would come to Israel, but he said that the timing was not in his area of prerogatives. That was for the Father to say. Nevertheless he said, "I have this authority." He explained further in verse 8, "You shall receive power when the Holy Spirit has come upon you; and you shall be My witnesses both in Jerusalem, and in all Judea and Samaria, and even to the remotest part of the earth."

THE TRINITY AT WORK

He authorizes us as witnesses for him today. He is the one who gives you the opportunity when you aren't expecting it at work or at school or at home. He is the one who makes two people meet, one who has the message, and one who needs the message. It's the authority of Christ; he sets it up. From His throne in heaven, he takes care of governing his church. He is head over all things in the church. Friend, he is directing your life as authority! He's the sovereign Christ.

Our Lord Jesus Christ by his ascension received authority to send the Holy Spirit, and the Holy Spirit in turn would send us with power. Jesus said in John 16: 7, "I tell you the truth, it is to your advantage that I go away; for if I do not go away, the Helper [who is the Holy Spirit] shall not come to you; but if I go, I will send Him to you."

The Scripture says in Ephesians 4 that when he ascended, "He gave gifts unto men." His ascension caused the Holy Spirit to give us gifts, "some apostles, some prophets, some evangelists, some pastors, some teachers for the equipping of the saints, for the work of the ministry." His ascension, then, started the chain of events which causes us to be a ministering people, to one another and to the world. As Elijah, before he was supernaturally received up into heaven, put his mantle on Elisha, so Jesus put his mantle on us, giving us the Spirit and the gifts by which to minister. A tremendous thing is the authority of Christ!

A NEW FUNCTION

Another door that opened for him when he ascended was that he became our intercessor. There is now a Man in heaven —a real human like us—at the right hand of God! Job had complained, "How can a man be right before God? . . . . For He is not a man as I am that I may answer Him, that we may go to court together. There is no umpire between us, who may lay his hand upon us both" (Job 9: 2, 32–33).

And he was right—until Jesus' ascension into heaven. But, praise God, now there is! As 1 Timothy 2: 5 says, "For there is one God, and one mediator also between God and men, the man Christ Jesus." He is our "advocate," the Scripture says, which means "our friend in court."

A NEW POSITION

The Apostle's Creed says, "He ascended into heaven and sitteth at the right hand of God,"—the place of power, the place of intimacy. There is Jesus Christ on your behalf, at the right hand of the Father. Often we get stuck in our sins or in our problems or in the situations of life that seem so difficult. But he is there to lift us. He is there, our advocate, the one who speaks well on our behalf, the one who watches over his church.

His hands are still outstretched in blessing! He is not only saving us *from* the uttermost, my friend, but he's got great plans for our lives to save us *to* the uttermost, that we might be all that we dream we might become. He is interceding so that we might see the fullness of God's plan worked out in our lives. Christ holds you and lifts you every day, all day long. It is the Lord Jesus looking over his church. He spares us and cares for us. I like what Ethel Waters says: "God don't sponsor no flops!"

OMNIPRESENT FOR ETERNITY

Then I see that by the ascension Christ became, for the first time, truly available. He is no longer geographically limited. The disciples had met him often during those forty days since his resurrection—we don't know how often, but at least ten times. Nevertheless, his ascension didn't threaten them with a fear of loneliness. It filled them with joy! They were at last getting the picture! "Lo, I am with you always, even to the end of the age," he said.

In later years when the Apostle Paul was in a discouraging time, when everyone had forsaken him, and he was alone in prison, do you know what he said? "The Lord stood with me." One writer put it, "When Jesus ascended into heaven, he did not leave the earth in the sense that he is no longer here. On the contrary, his ascension brought him closer to us than he could ever have been to his own contemporaries. He left in order that he might be nearer to us all. . . . He was taken away from among men in order that he might come to dwell within men."

CHRIST'S EARTHLY LIFE

Well, we've been through the baptism of Jesus when he was Spirit-empowered and anointed. We've looked at that glorious scene when he was tempted and defeated the temptor. We've looked at his choosing of the Twelve and training them to be with him to do his will. We found him at the Transfiguration, the inner glory breaking forth in splendor. We wept with him to the cross, where he saved us from our sins, and where two men during the very act of crucifixion became believers and recipients of his salvation. We entered the empty tomb. We saw how this was the climax of his ministry. The Old and New Testaments prophesied that He would rise from the dead. And we've seen his glorious ascension, Jesus transferred into that new realm to take up a new ministry for us. These are the crucial events in the life of Christ!

CHRIST'S HEAVENLY LIFE RESUMED

Of Christ, having ended all these glorious acts on our behalf, Philippians 2: 9 says, "Therefore also God highly exalted . . . and bestowed on Him the name which is above every name, that at the name of Jesus every knee should bow . . . and that every tongue should confess that Jesus Christ is Lord, to the glory of God the Father."

And most amazing of all, with authority and power he went back to heaven to prepare a place for you and me (John 14: 2). Hebrews 6: 20 says that he entered into heaven "as a forerunner for us!"

Surely the implications of the ascension of Jesus Christ must have the same effect on us that they had on the first disciples: "with great joy," they "were continually in the temple praising God."

Norval Geldenhuys says in *The New International Com-*

mentary: The Gospel of Luke, "So grand and mighty was the revelation . . . that the disciples spontaneously worshiped him. . . . And just as the gospel history commenced in 'an atmosphere of worship and joy, so it ends here in the last words of Luke on a note of unparalleled joy and fervor of divine worship."

> *Praise God from whom all blessings flow;*
> *Praise him, all creatures here below;*
> *Praise him above, ye heavenly hosts;*
> *Praise Father, Son, and Holy Ghost.*

Study Questions

Review the text as you answer the questions.

1. What did Christ's ascension end, and what did it begin?

2. Give the historical facts of the ascension: when it happened, where, how, who witnessed it, and what was said by whom.

3. Give reasons why the ascension might have started a "ticker tape parade" in heaven.

4. "His ascension . . . started a chain of events." Name everything new you can think of which could happen now that Christ was ascended.

5. What benefits does Christ's ascension give to you personally?

II

And now we come to what is for your life, one of the deepest, highest, noblest, and most encouraging truths of all. As Christ ascended into heaven, so you also have ascended; and you, too, are seated in the heavenlies in a seat of authority and dignity and honor.

This isn't something that will happen some day, but in the meantime we just grovel around. Notice the tense of the verbs in Ephesians 2: 5: "We were dead in your trespasses and sins." That was in your preconversion days.

"But God, who is rich in mercy, made us alive together with Christ." Here is a statement of your identification with him, that when God put life back into the dead body of Jesus, he counted it as happening to you, too. "And [He] raised us up with Him . . . and seated us with Him in the heavenly places in Christ Jesus" (Eph. 2: 1, 4–6).

IDENTIFICATION WITH CHRIST

Notice three times the words *with Christ, with Him, with Him.* Like the paper in the book, everything that happened to Christ, happened to us. Our minds are so locked into time that we think in terms of history, and we wonder how we could have ascended with Christ when we weren't even born yet. But God thinks by *truth,* and time is no problem to him. Don't limit his workings to what you understand! "For My thoughts are not your thoughts, Neither are your ways My ways," declares the Lord. "For as the heavens are higher than the earth, so are My ways higher than your ways, and My thoughts than your thoughts" (Isa. 55: 8–9).

I remember the first time my wife Anne and I were struck by the fact of our being seated in the heavenlies with Christ. In discouraging moments sometimes we'd said to each other, "Keep looking up!" This time I said to her, "Keep looking down!" We loved it. It gave us a new sense of understanding where we truly are, where God has placed us. We are heavenly people, not earthly. We have a lofty position. We are truly "in Christ!" We have mounted up "with wings as eagles," who nest 'way up high.

And spiritually, there doesn't need to be any fear of high places, or fear of falling. It's simply a matter of identification with our Lord Jesus, of stature, of privileged position, of unearned honor, even of the thrill of being totally in, totally accepted. "Blessed be the God and Father of our Lord Jesus Christ, who hath blessed us with all spiritual blessings in heavenly places in Christ: . . . To the praise of the glory of his grace, wherein he hath made us accepted in the beloved" (Eph. 1: 3, 6, KJV).

Your Horizons Expanded

Being seated in the heavenlies in Christ is also a matter of vision. "The heavens are higher than the earth, and My thoughts are higher than your thoughts." That's what the Lord said back in the Old Testament, centuries before the "mystery" of Gentiles being included in one Body of Christ was ever unveiled. But now, very humbly and reverently think of the implications of your being ascended with Christ. Your position, your viewpoint, your thinking, your conversation should be truly lofty! John 3: 31–32 says, "He who comes from above is above all, he who is of the earth is from the earth and speaks of the earth. He who comes from heaven is above all. What he has seen and heard, of that he bears witness."

Do you think like an earthling, talk like an earthling? Then you don't even realize who you are and where you are! The whole second chapter of 1 Corinthians was written to tell us that the minds of "natural" men naturally have to stay down here on earth, but that God has given to us the mind of Christ. Part of our identifying with him is that we can share his mentality. Seated with him, we see things from his point of view. Listen to the way the Living Bible says it: "The spiritual man has insight into everything. . . . Strange as it seems, we Christians actually do have within us a portion of the very thoughts and mind of Christ" (1 Cor. 2: 15–16, LB).

NEGATIVES IN PERSPECTIVE

Now, since this is true that you have been raised with Christ and are seated in the heavenlies in him, what about your feelings of inferiority, your anxieties, your worries, your unrest? All those situations concerning our earthly life are way down there below. They're small and insignificant. They have no grip on us after all.

We talk about worldly Christians. What is a worldly Christian? He's one who lives and thinks and acts and desires down on the level of the world, with all the true worldlings. The worldly Christian has resurrection life within; he has this wonderful position in Christ, but he isn't living like it.

So the Lord pleads with us, "If [or since] then you have been raised up with Christ, keep seeking the things above, where Christ is, seated at the right hand of God" (Col. 3: 1).

Follow the way the Living Bible says it: "Let heaven fill your thoughts; don't spend your time worrying about things down here. You should have as little desire for this world as a dead person does. Your real life is in heaven with Christ and God" (Col. 3: 2–3, LB).

HAVE HEAVENLY CHARACTERISTICS

Have you ever seen a bird covered with mud? Obviously if you did, the bird would be sick, dying, or dead. It would certainly be unnatural. His sphere is higher; he lives above that kind of contact. Have you seen an earthworm covered with mud? Certainly; why not?

So we should never expect natural men without Christ to show spiritual understanding or to display the fruits of the Spirit. They just can't fly!

But when we see a Christian with mud on him, with the anxieties and cares and mentality of this world about him, my friend, he's sick. God never intended him to be like that, and he doesn't need to be.

So there we are. And we can say to one another, "Keep looking down. It all looks good from his vantage point, being ascended with Christ."

Have you ever gone to the airport on an overcast day, a bit miserable, cold and gloomy. You boarded the plane, and it taxied and took off. Up you went through the clouds, and suddenly you burst out into the sunshine. There was the glory of the sun.

Oh, friend, let's live with Jesus, once the Christ of Bethlehem and Nazareth, but now the Christ at the right hand of God, far above all, where the glory is!

"Behold, [he says], I stand at the door and knock. If anyone hears My voice and opens the door, I will come in to him, and will dine with him, and he with Me. He who overcomes, I will grant to him to sit down with Me on My throne, as I also overcame and sat down with My Father on His throne. He who has an ear, let him hear what the Spirit says to the churches" (Rev. 3: 20–22).

Study Questions

Review the text as you answer these questions.

1. When were you "made alive," according to the accounting books of God? When were you "raised" and "seated in heavenly places"?

2. What should be the differences in the "earthly person" and the person who is "in Christ"? List the differences this should make. What effect should they have on your life's goals and achievements?

3. How will the believer who is enjoying his heavenly position view problems? Has this been your experience?

4. What should be the healthy Christian's normal mind-set and attitude from day to day?

5. What are the traps that can keep us from true normality and health? Spend time in prayer about these things.